Mocollop Castle, Co Waterford

THE CASTLES
OF SOUTH MUNSTER

Mike Salter

FOLLY PUBLICATIONS

ACKNOWLEDGEMENTS

The illustrations in this book are mostly the product of the author's own site surveys since 1971. Plans redrawn from his field notebooks are mostly reproduced to scales of 1:400 for keeps, tower houses, stronghouses, etc, and 1:800 for courtyard castles and bawns, whilst large sites are shown at 1:2000. The photos of Castle Lough and Killagha, and one view each of Kilcrea and Lismore appearing on pages 69 and 11 respectively were taken by Ian Rennie, who also drove on the 2003 expedition and checked parts of the text. The photo of Dromaneen is reproduced by courtesy of the Department of the Environment, Heritage and Local Government. Thanks are due to Eamon Cody and the staff of the archaeological section of that department in Dublin for allowing access to the archaeological records and providing much help, information and advice. About a dozen of the drawings are at least partly based on material contained in their records. Thanks are also due to Pennie Gillis, who drove on the 1982 expedition, Paul Adkins for solving computer set-up problems, Helen Thomas for checking the text, and the staff of the Bodleian Library at Oxford, especially the map section.

AUTHOR'S NOTES

This book is one of a series of volumes superseding the author's previous work Castles and Stronghouses of Ireland, published in 1993 and now out of print. It is part of a series of books about castles throughout Britain and Ireland, all in a similar style with plans on a set of common scales allowing useful comparisons of sizes, wall thicknesses, etc. It is recommended that visitors use the Ordnance Survey 1:50,000 scale maps to locate the monuments, grid references being given in the gazetteers, along with codes indicating which castles can be visited or viewed from public rights of way (see page 13). The book is intended as a portable field guide giving as much information and illustrative material as possible in a book of modest size, weight and price, especially providing material about buildings not properly described elsewhere in print. The aim has been to give some basic information about owners or custodians of castles, but no attempt has been made to provide detailed genealogical histories. Ghost stories, myths and legends are not normally included, and personalities later than the 1690s are generally only mentioned if of importance to an understanding of a building's development or state of ruination.

All dimensions are given in metres and usually refer to the size of the building at or near ground level, but above the plinth if there is one. Most towers and hall-houses will be smaller than the quoted dimensions higher up because of the external batter of the walls. The majority of the measurements quoted were personally taken on site by the author. On plans the original work is shown black, post-1800 work is stippled and alterations and additions of intermediate periods are shown hatched. Each level is called a storey, sleeping and storage lofts tucked under vaults being treated as full storeys, and the basement being the first or lowest storey with its floor at or near ground level unless mentioned as otherwise. An attic room entirely within the height of a gabled roof is usually mentioned as an extra level additional to the number of storeys given.

ABOUT THE AUTHOR

Mike Salter is 50 and has been a professional writer and publisher since 1988. He is particularly interested in the planning and layout of medieval buildings and has a huge collection of plans of castles and churches he has measured during tours (mostly by bicycle and motorcycle) throughout all parts of the British Isles since 1968. Wolverhampton born and bred, Mike now lives in an old cottage beside the Malvern Hills. His other interests include walking, maps, railways, board games, morris dancing and playing percussion instruments and calling folk dances with an occasional folk group.

First published January 2004. Copyright 2004 Mike Salter
Folly Publications, Folly Cottage, 151 West Malvern Rd, Malvern, Worcs WR14 4AY
Printed by Aspect Design, 89 Newtown Rd, Malvern, Worcs WR14 2PD.

Clonea Castle, Co Waterford

CONTENTS

A map of surviving castles appears inside the front cover.

BRIEF HISTORICAL INTRODUCTION

Not long before the Normans arrived in Ireland in 1169 Munster had been divided into two kingdoms. Deas Mumha or South Munster was ruled by the MacCarthys, who submitted to King Henry II of England in 1171 in expectation of support against their rivals, the O'Briens of North Munster. King Henry promptly granted much of present day Cork and Kerry to Robert FitzStephen and Milo de Cogan, and the MacCarthys tendency to quarrel amongst themselves made it possible for these Norman lords to establish themselves in South Munster. The Gaelic system of tanistry or choosing an heir from any of a chief's male relatives led to much infighting amongst the clans, a weakness the Normans were quick to exploit, since nearly every chief had a rival amongst his own clan. Robert FitzStephen's share eventually passed to two nephews, Maurice FitzGerald and Philip de Barry, from whom descended the two most important Norman families in South Munster, the Geraldine earls of Desmond, whose main seat was at Tralee, and the Barrymores, based at Barryscourt until they transferred to Castle Lyons in the 1620s. The de Cogans acquired by marriage lands which had been taken by the Prendergasts and the de Courcys managed to similarly acquire a lordship around Kinsale, whilst the Le Poers (later anglicised as Power) took much of County Waterford. In 1261 Fineen MacCarthy defeated the FitzGeralds near Kenmare and destroyed many Norman settlements until he was killed in a fight with the De Courcys near Kinsale and this heralded a gradual resumption of power by the Irish chiefs. The MacCarthys gradually adopted Norman ways and eventually recovered much of Muskerry by marriage, intrigue and other means. English power declined in Ireland during the early 14th century and the arrival of the Black Death in 1349 caused further problems. Some lords went to England in the mid 15th century to fight in the Wars of the Roses, and the MacCarthys soon capitalised on their absence, taking over Cloghroe and Blarney, whilst the weakened de Cogans surrendered their lordship to the Earl of Desmond in return for his protection.

Gerald, later 16th Earl of Desmond, was obliged while in prison in England to mortgage lands to the St Leger family, but a junior branch of the Desmond FitzGeralds had a claim on the lands and led a revolt in 1569. This eventually led to a widespread full scale rebellion lasting from 1579 until the capture and execution of the earl in 1583, resulting in many of the FitzGeralds and their supporters being forfeited. Queen Elizabeth now pursued a policy under which the chiefs where obliged to surrender the lands held by them in trust for their whole clan and have them regranted by the queen to them personally. Those who resisted were liable for forfeiture as and when the Lord Deputy was strong enough to enforce this. The result was that English courtiers like Edmund Spenser and Sir Walter Raleigh were able to obtain large estates which were then settled with Protestant tenant families. Small scale Spanish invasions and campaigns in the south in 1598 and 1601 by the Catholic earls of Tyrone and Tyconnell forced the issue and led to the final defeat of the Catholic rebels at Kinsale. Cormac MacDermot MacCarthy managed with great skill not to join either side, but the other lords all took part in the conflict and lost or gained lands and influence depending on their choice. Many of the remaining FitzGeralds and the O'Sullivans and several other western clans were defeated and their lands confiscated. By the 1620s one of the greatest landowners of the rich central lands was Richard Boyle, then created Earl of Cork (but some years previously hardly more than a penniless clerk), but the St Legers as Presidents of Munster also had great influence.

During the wars of the 1640s some of the lords who had lost lands tried to regain them. Lord Inchiquin (an O'Brien), the Earl of Cork's son Lord Broghill, and Sir Charles Vavasour led the loyal (or Parliamentary) forces in the area, and Lord Castlehaven led the Confederate Catholics, who were, in effect, Royalists. The final blow to the Gaelic Catholic cause was Cromwell's invasion of 1649 and the subsequent widespread confiscation of lands in the mid 1650s which were all handed over to Protestants, many of the settlers being former officers of Cromwell's army. In the 1690s there was another round of confiscations of lands belonging to supporters of the defeated and exiled James II, the MacCarthy Earl of Clancarty being the chief casualty in this respect.

Kilmurry Castle, Kerry

Crooke Castle, Waterford

Lohort Castle, Co Cork

Although sometimes able to withstand infantry attacks during the wars of the 16th and 17th centuries, the Irish tower houses were unable to resist cannonfire and were usually quickly surrendered when bombarded. Although available to the Lord Deputy appointed by the Crown, cannon do not seem to have been widespread in Ireland during the 16th century except in government forts and town defences. There is little evidence of them being deployed at the seats of the great lords except in times of war, and hardly any of the castles contain gunports suitable for firing cannon out of. Cannon large enough to smash castle walls were very expensive and few lords could have afforded them, although by the late 16th century muskets and pistols were common enough and castles of that period are equipped with small loops suitable for the discharge of these weapons. Cromwell, equipped with a modern and efficient siege train of artillery, was quickly able to reduce all castles that offered resistance during his campaigns of 1649-50 and that heralded the end of castles in all parts of Britain functioning as privately owned defensible residences. Forts of later periods were state-run institutions with a purely military purpose. By the 18th century most of the Irish castles not burnt or blown up during the wars of 1640-52 and 1689-1691 had been abandoned in favour of more modern country houses.

ARCHITECTURAL INTRODUCTION

Forts with earth ramparts with a hedge or wooden palisade on top or with walls of limestone blocks laid without mortar were common in Ireland in the Dark Ages but castles as the Normans knew them were almost unknown prior their invasion in 1169-70. The Normans seem to have met with little resistance in the southern part of Munster, and the very few examples of mottes or artificial earthen mounds in the area with concerns us in this book mostly lie in County Waterford. Mottes bore wooden towers with palisaded courts around them and were often accompanied by a bailey platform to accommodate a timber hall and other buildings such as barns and stables, but there is only one instance of a motte with a bailey in Waterford, plus a single possible example in Cork. There are also a few instances of moated platforms which mark sites of undefended manor houses.

The gazetteers of this book describe over 300 fortified buildings of mortared stone. The vast majority of them date from the early 15th century to the mid 17th century, i.e. the late medieval and Tudor and Stuart periods. Less than twenty of the sites have standing walls likely to be earlier than the 1420s. For some sites there is a record of work done in the 13th or 14th centuries, or circumstantial evidence of a early castle existing by then, but there are either no remains at all, or only buildings of much later date. Because of so much destruction during Ireland's turbulent past reliable records of the construction or reconstruction of Irish castles infrequently survive. Those records that do remain tend to relate to work from the 1550s onwards, i.e the last hundred years of the 450 year period during which residences of mortared stone capable of at least some measure of defence were being built in Ireland. They also tend to relate to works carried out by English-speaking lords and state officials rather than the Gaelic-speaking chiefs. The result is that we can only guess at when most of the surviving buildings might have been constructed, using certain clues like masonry techniques, plan forms, wall thicknesses, whether vaulting is used and if so how the vaults have been formed, and the form of openings, especially windows, where they survive intact.

Glanworth Castle, Co Cork

Clashmelcon Castle, Co Kerry

Liscarroll Castle, Co Cork

Blarney Castle, Co Cork

The city of Waterford is thought to have had stone defences during the Viking period and upon the circuit of the walls is a strong circular keep known as Reginald's tower which may date from King John's reign, i.e. c1200, and probably replaces a motte. Inchiquin in Co Cork has an even larger and more massive circular keep containing just one upper chamber over a dark basement. Five other round towers in County Waterford are probably all 16th century tower houses, as are Carrickabrick in Co Cork and Barrow in Co Kerry. Certainly none of them predate the 1420s, but there is a circular tower which may go back to the 13th century at Parkavonear in Kerry. Dungarvan in Co Waterford has a polygonal shell keep with a retaining wall built around a motte which may also go back to King John's reign, whilst the rectangular bailey there with one large circular corner tower and a gatehouse with twin U-shaped towers flanking the passage seems to be the product of his son Henry III's expenditure in the 1260s and 70s. Of about that time are the remains of the expanded town wall system at Waterford, with several round towers surviving, and town walls were also begun during the 13th century at Cork and Youghal.

In this and subsequent paragraphs places marked (K) are in Co Kerry and places marked with a (W) are in Co Waterford, and all others lie in Co Cork. Liscarroll has a fairly complete late 13th century courtyard castle with circular corner towers and a rectangular gatehouse. There are more fragmentary remains of similar castles at Buttevant and Kilbolane, whilst the court at Glanworth was originally without flanking towers but had a gatehouse on one side, a hall and chamber block on another and a detached keep. The plain rectangular courts without any towers at Kilmaclenine and Leitrim are also 13th century, or perhaps 14th century, a century to which very few Irish castle buildings are attributed. The small but massively walled court at Ardea (K) is also likely to be early.

Bawn at Kilmaclenine, Co Cork   *Ballyplymoth Castle, Kerry*

Ballyderown is a hall-house, i.e. a self-contained defensible hall block without significant outer defences. It appears to have originally contained just a single magnificent chamber over a dark lower room, although that raises the problem of where its lord would have slept as there is no obvious private room. The smaller and less massive hall houses at Castle Barrett and Licklash were each later provided with a tier small private chambers in a tower-like wing. There are slight remains of another hall house at Carrigrohane. Two other hall houses, a modest one at Ballymacphilip and a huge one at Ballycarbery (K) both have vaulting and appear to be 15th century buildings continuing this tradition. That at Ballycarbery certainly had a separate private room at one end of the hall. A possible early hall and chamber block also exist on one side of the later bawn at Barryscourt.

Nearly all of the castles built in Ireland during the 15th and 16th century were of the type now known as a tower house. They are widespread in Scotland and the northern parts of England and seem to have been generally regarded as a suitable form of residence in the 14th, 15th and 16th centuries for lesser landowners needing a measure of defensibility in strife-torn areas where raiding was endemic. In England only a few of the later medieval lordly residences (fortified or not) away from the border regions featured a tower house, but in Ireland the type was almost universally adopted, regardless of rank. For the defence of the Pale around Dublin in Leinster Henry VI encouraged the building of small towers by offering a cash subsidy for their construction but it is doubtful if this had much effect on what went on in Munster. It seems that the greatest magnates such as the earls of Desmond and their lieutenants the seneschals of Imokilly began building impressive new tower houses in the 1420s and that everyone else eventually followed suit. The towers vary quite a lot in size and massiveness depending on the status and wealth of the person the tower was originally meant to accommodate, or the importance attached to defending a place of strategic importance such as a river crossing. Sometimes there was a need to impress the local inhabitants after an estate or district changed hands, whether by marriage, purchase, inheritance, an exchange, or blatant military conquest.

Of about 400 castellated buildings dating from c1200 to c1650 of which there are still standing remains in Cork, Kerry and Waterford, about 350 are tower houses dating from the second half of the period under discussion. Ten tower houses are still inhabited, half of them in a much modified or cut-down form, and six others are roofed but not occupied as dwellings. All the rest are ruins ranging from a complete shell to a mere fragment beside a pile of fallen debris. The majority of the towers now stand alone, but quite a number lie next to later houses or farm buildings, although in some cases these too are ruinous.

About twenty tower houses have a fairly well preserved attached court known as a bawn and there are about another twenty towers with more fragmentary remains of bawns or their flanking turrets or bastions (usually referred to as flankers). Most of the bawns are nearly level rectangular courts of modest size (rarely more than 45m long), with walls occasionally up to 1.6m thick and 6m high, although the later examples tend to have walls only about 1m thick and 4m high. Good examples are at Castlemartyr (where there is a second substantial rectangular tower), Barryscourt, Ross (K), and Ballincollig (where the central tower is little more than a lookout post or status symbol). The large bawns of late date at Blarney and Dromaneen are hard to take seriously as defensive enclosures, despite their provision for flanking fire, and are more in the nature of ornamental walled gardens. Bawns often had flankers at least at some of the corners, usually circular structures up to 6m in diameter, often with two levels of gunloops, making a date after 1550 likely.

Bawns were sometimes built on their own without a dominating tower house, and these examples are slightly more likely to have some form of primitive gatehouse. More elaborately planned and defended gatehouses only occur in the handful of earlier medieval castles already described. Bawn gateways were closed with wooden doors secured with a drawbar and there are no examples with portcullis grooves. Some of the headland sites in SW Cork have a ditch in front of the bawn wall that was must have been crossed by a drawbridge or sliding bridge but none of the inland bawns has any evidence of a drawbridge at the gateway. Openings in the outer walls of bawns and the occasional provision of staircases, fireplaces, ovens, latrines and other small mural chambers suggest the former presence of lean-to buildings up to two storeys high set against the walls, although these never survive except for occasional fragments or foundations, or buildings inserted at a rather later date.

Window at Ballymalis

Ballyclogh Castle

Ballycarbery Castle

Barnahely Castle, Co Cork

Gunloops at Carriganass, Co Cork

There are enough variations in the planning and features of the tower houses to make them interesting, but some arrangements and features are very common indeed. As already mentioned there are one or two circular 16th century examples and a few are square or nearly so in plan, but the majority of the tower houses are rectangular, usually without any projections, although about twenty examples have a small projecting turret to contain latrines or a wing containing extra private rooms. Many of the towers have a graceful batter but some simply have battered bases and then rise vertically. Nearly all the towers have one end wall thickened so as to be able to contain a tier of small private mural chambers and a staircase in one corner. The lobby of the entrance at ground level is usually protected by a murder-hole in the floor of the lowest mural chamber. A small group of 15th century towers in SW Cork has separate entrances one above the other to the lowest two levels with the spiral stair starting from the second storey. Many of the towers have a spiral stair starting from the second storey level but usually there is a straight mural stair running up to it from the ground level entrance. The entrance was usually closed by a wooden door opening inwards and often there was a hinged iron grille called a yett opening outwards, a hole in the door jamb being used for a chain to secure the yett. Tower houses rarely had portcullises but there were a few 15th century examples in Cork, notably Ballynacarriga, Ballycrenane, Inchicrenane and Oldcourt.

Although the smaller towers sometimes only had four habitable levels, there were often five in the larger towers. In this book each level is called a storey, even if it was no more than a storage loft or sleeping attic lighted by a single loop in an end wall and squeezed under a stone vault. In this part of Ireland five storey towers usually have vaults over the second and fourth storeys, and consequently the third and fifth storey rooms were the grandest, although in some towers the vaulted fourth storey is a lofty enough room to be a proper living space rather than just a dark loft. Vaults may be round-arched, segmental or pointed and where there are two they may be of different forms or orientated differently within the building. Later medieval vaults were usually laid over mats of wickerwork laid on timber frames and often show signs of these mats.

Sometimes there are extra mural rooms in the other walls apart from those in the one thick end wall. The haunches of vaults are sometimes left hollow for use as passages or rooms. In the upper parts of Castle Cooke both end walls contain chambers, providing a number of private rooms, some of them quite spacious. A common arrangement is for two latrines at different levels to descend into a single chute which is nearly always towards the end of one of the long walls. Where wall-walks still have their parapets (many were knocked off as an easy way of making towers indefensible) they normally have tall double stepped merlons, a peculiarly Irish fashion used across the country throughout the tower house building period. The roofs might be of slabs, slates or thatch, and often contained attic rooms lighted by small windows in the gables set within the wall-walks.

Windows in Irish towers tend to be narrow. On the upper levels the lights may be paired and on the topmost level they may be tall enough for a transom to be provided, but the individual lights still remain narrow. Consequently the iron stanchions or grilles used on elsewhere in Europe were less common on Irish towers, although they were used in the 17th century fortified houses. For the sake of brevity in the gazetteers only those windows with ogival heads, hoodmoulds or other decorative features such as carved or sunk spandrels beside ogival heads are mentioned specifically and other windows not fully described will have square-headed (or occasionally round-headed) lights. Generally these tall narrow windows were provided with internal shutters rather than glass. Occasionally a stone hanging eye for mounting the upper pivots of a window shutter or door still survives. A speciality of Irish tower houses, never found in their Scottish and English counterparts, is to provide loops (often at third storey level) that pierce the actual corner of the building itself. Minard (K) and Castle Barrett have much rarer examples of this being done with a two-light window, the mullion forming the corner of the tower. The embrasures of main room upper windows sometimes have seats. The rere-arches are often semi-circular or segmental, although lintels are often used, especially lower down and for the narrower embrasures of loops of mural chambers and passages.

All the arrangements and features of tower houses described so far can occur at any period from the 1440s to the 1640s. There are, however, certain features that seem to have begun to be used more commonly from about the 1550s, and these help us to decide whether a tower is likely to be early or late during the two hundred year period of their being in fashion. The only towers to contain gunports suitable for mounting cannon are one or two specialised purely military blockhouses such as Blackrock, but many of the towers and the flanking turrets of their bawns contain small round or square holes or gunloops suitable for the discharge of muskets or pistols. Such weapons existed in Ireland in the 1490s but it is unlikely that Irish towers and bawns were equipped for systematic defence by firearms before the 1520s, and the majority of the buildings so equipped are probably of the period 1550-1620. Gunloops are often found on either side of windows or loops, opening off the same embrasure. Raheen and Ballynamona have the rare and very ingenious features of gable-shaped recesses against all four sides with a gunloop in the apex of each gable so as to completely command the whole of the base of the building. Mashanglass and Carrignacurra have an equally rare feature, triangular casemates containing gunloops and themselves flanked by gunloops in the main tower, the triangular shape ensuring that there was no dead ground where an assailant could shelter. At Carrignacurra this feature must date from some time between the 1540s, when arrowhead-shaped bastions were first introduced into Ireland, and 1584, when a document describing the tower specifically mentions the spur. The presence of flanking towers with gunloops also indicates a late date for bawns, and indeed most of them probably date from the mid to late 16th century.

Bartizan at Ballynacarriga

River front of Lismore Castle

Towers with gunloops also tend to have fireplaces in their upper rooms, and consequently there are chimney stacks at the top, those on the sidewalls often partly or entirely impeding access round the wall-walk. Indeed a few late towers did not have full circuits of wall-walks. The evidence suggests that the lower and intermediate levels of 15th century Irish towers were unheated and that where the topmost room lay over an upper vault it had a central hearth or brazier with a louvre in the roof to allow smoke to escape. This top room, by far the largest because of the internal thinning of the walls, was usually the main public hall, the chief's private room being further down the tower. This is the opposite of the usual English and Scottish preference for a public room over the cellar with more private rooms higher up and is perhaps a consequence of the Gaelic chiefs' closer relationship with their clansmen, compared with the elitism of English lords.

There are several instances of upper fireplaces (often with joggled lintels and side brackets to help take the thrust of the walling above) bearing initials of owners with dates, but these are misleading, since they often only refer to minor later alterations and not the original period of construction of the main building, as at Barryscourt, where the year given is 1586. Many mid to late 15th century towers seem to have been modernised with fireplaces and gunloops in the late 16th and early 17th centuries, and the huge L-plan tower at Blarney appears to be the work of three separate periods, the wing having originally been a small separate tower. Irish towers rarely have rooms for one obvious specific purpose such as a kitchen or chapel, but a room in the wing at Blarney was later made into a kitchen, whilst a room in the wing at Barryscourt is fitted out as a chapel.

Plain mullioned windows with lights wider than the tall ogival-headed late medieval type ones also became fashionable in the late 16th century. A lot of the towers have bartizans or projecting turrets at two diagonally opposite corners. These usually contain gunloops flanking the walls and between the corbels supporting them are machicolation slots for dropping or firing missiles upon assailants. These also appear to be a late feature, certainly so if gunloops are present. A particularly Irish trait is the use of tall narrow inverted pyramidal corbels to support the bartizans. At Blarney there is a continuous machicolated parapet probably of the 1590s set upon such corbels around three quarters of the tower, and there is another, similarly with a gap on one side, at Lohort. Box-machicolations or projections off the parapet of the wall-walk to protect the entrance far below were common throughout the tower house building period. Ballymalis (K) typifies a number of late towers of the last two decades of the 16th century. There none of the main rooms is vaulted, and the bartizans are of a roofed-in type in the form of projecting chambers (still will machicolations) at the third storey level of the tower. Bartizans of this type also occur at Kilmeedy and Sheanmore (W).

In the medieval period walls were often whitewashed both inside and out, thus making the best of the limited light admitted through the narrow windows. The lowest room (it was rarely subdivided in Irish tower houses) was generally used for storage but the living rooms above often had built-in seats in the window embrasures. These rooms might sometimes have wall-paintings of biblical, allegorical or heroic scenes, or tapestries or other hangings with similar motifs. Carpets were only introduced in the late 16th century, before which those floors not formed of planks laid on massive beams were made of rammed earth or clay. All the floors were covered with rushes changed occasionally as thought necessary. Cooking was done on the main fire since specific kitchens were rare in Irish tower houses. English and Spanish nobles on military campaigns in Ireland found the local cuisine primitive compared with what they were used to back home.

The sort of privacy we all now take for granted hardly existed in a medieval castle. Even nobles often had attendants sleeping in the same room or in a passage outside, although the lordly bed would usually be screened or curtained off. Furniture was sparse and of the simplest kind until the 17th century. Only the chief and his immediate family were likely to have individual chairs, but the hall would contain tables and benches. Also suitable for seating were the chests within which clothes, plate, and other valuables were kept. A notable feature of the towers is the number of lockers within the walls, nearly every window embrasure having one in some of the towers.

The defeat and forfeiture of the earl of Desmond and his followers in the 1580s led to a new plantation of parts of Munster with Protestant settlers. Some of them preferred to dwell in new houses which were more like the Elizabethan houses of England with their spacious rooms filled with light from large mullion-and-transom windows. However, they still felt a need to retain some defensive features such as gunloops and machicolations. Before long some of the Gaelic chiefs began to build such houses in imitation of them. The stronghouse of c1600 at Mallow had large rooms with big windows with a wide staircase of wood in a back wing and a lack of vaulting, but with gunloops under the windows. The main block has two polygonal corner turrets and the stair wing on one side and the entrance wing on the other produce a cruciform plan which was copied (without the extra turrets) in other stronghouses of c1610-45 at Ballyduff (W) (which has a small bawn with flankers), Sleady (W), Kilmaclenine, and Ightermurragh. Tickincor (W) is a T-plan, i.e. it has a stair wing but not the extra entrance wing on the other side. Also T-planned is Kilmurry (K), a hybrid building being a stronghouse in layout and features with the entrance and stair in the wing, but with uniquely massive walls for such a building.

Coppinger's Court has a stair wing at the back and two wings facing the bawn at the front. The bawn had little defensive value but the house is impressively machicolated on the side walls of each wing. The end wall which is all that remains at Lisgriffin is also machicolated, whilst Donagh MacCarthy's great unfinished house at Kanturk with the main block flanked by gunloops in four square corner towers has corbels for machicolations round the whole building. The very similar houses of Monkstown and Mountlong also have four corner towers, the former having a machicolated bartizan on the outermost corner of each tower. There are also bartizans of a crude type upon the T-shaped Reendisert Court (K). Castle Lyons as redeveloped from an early tower as the Barry chief seat in the 1620s differs from the others in that it had four ranges laid out somewhat irregularly and including work of different periods, set around a central court. The house appears to have been fortified in the 1640s with various outworks. Two buildings dating from after the wars, Ballyannan of the 1650s and Aghadown of the 1670s perpetuate the tradition for flankers but without actually providing them with gunloops. Ballyannan has round tower towers at diagonally opposite corners, a layout more typically Scottish than Irish, while Aghadown had two arrowhead shaped corner wings. Other late 17th century buildings are thinly walled and without any castellated features, thus bringing us to the end of the period of construction of fortified residences in Ireland.

ACCESS TO THE CASTLES

The following codes appear after the O.S. grid references in the gazetteers. They give only an indication since access arrangements may change from time to time, as may the amount of vegetation obscuring distant views, whilst some monuments may only be open during the summer months. Sites not given a code lie on private land and can only be seen by obtaining prior permission from the landowners. Only occasionally will a courteous request for access by those with a genuine interest in ancient buildings be refused outright, although some owners may forbid visitors to enter ruins considered precarious. Visitors should in all cases close any gates that they need to open, ensure that their dogs do not cause any kind of nuisance to the farmers or their animals, and generally follow the maxim of taking away only photographs and leaving behind nothing but footprints.

A - Free access on foot to the whole site at any time. Most sites in state care.
B - Free access on foot at any time to the exterior only. Mostly sites in state care.
C - Private, but clearly visible from public road, path, or other public open space.
D - Private, but distant view usually possible from road, path or other open space.
E - Open to the public (fee usually payable) during certain hours (at least in summer).
G - Private, but fairly easy courtesy access is currently normally possible.
H - Buildings in use as hotels, shops, museums, etc. Exterior access usually possible.

GAZETTEER OF CASTLES OF COUNTY CORK

AGHADOWN   W049332   D

Only the thin west wall with a fireplace remains of a house said to have been built by the Beecher family in 1670, probably to replace an older castle nearby, and occupied by them until the 19th century. The house had four spear-head shaped corner flankers, the western two of which still stand two storeys high with a string course between the levels, although there are no gunloops. The NW flanker has a square basement room. The SW flanker has a hexagonal chimney stack over fireplaces in the acute outer angle.

AGHAMARTA   W766608   C

Parts of this tower collapsed in 1839 along with most of a spiral stair in a circular turret added at the SW corner. There are three storeys with the second vaulted. It was held by the Nugents in the 16th century and is 8.6m wide. There may originally have been small rooms beyond the existing thin west wall, giving a length of about 13.5m.

AGHERNE   W895929

The wide embrasure on the north side of a tower 11.3m long by 8.8m wide was later partly blocked by a crosswall carrying two vaults. The western room was made into a boiler-house in the 19th century and the eastern room has been subdivided. About 15m to the east is a later second tower measuring 8.5m by 6.8m but with the western part of the south wall thickened by an extra 1.1m to contain a spiral stair reached from outside. The tower contains a cellar and loft under a vault. The upper parts of both towers have been removed. They formed the southern corners of a court corresponding to the present coachyard of the early 19th century house north of the eastern tower. An old doorway has been reset in the modern wall linking them. This FitzGerald castle guarding a ford over the Bride was garrisoned against the English in 1580. It was later sold to Richard Boyle.

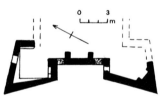

Plan of house at Aghadown

House at Aghadown

Ballea Castle

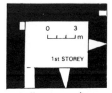

Ardintenant: plans

Aghamarta Castle

ARDINTENANT or WHITE CASTLE V949310

A 15th century O'Mahony four storey tower measuring 10m by 8.5m lies on the NW side of a ringfort 38m across with evidence of a bawn wall which was flanked on the south by a rectangular turret containing three levels of small rooms under a vault, the top storey having a spiral stair up to the top. The main tower has south-facing doorways on the lowest two levels. From the upper doorway a stair rises to the SE corner and then a spiral stair leads to the roof. The top storey windows have seats in the embrasures. The second storey has a passage leading to a latrine in the NE corner.

BALLEA W709631 D

This tower on a cliff above the Owenboy River measures 14.2m long by 8.6m wide over walls 2m thick and was probably built by the FitzGeralds after they obtained the lands here from the de Cogans in 1439. The remaining features, including window heads with step-ended hoodmoulds lying loose in the garden, suggest that it was remodelled as a three storey L-plan stronghouse in the early 17th century. A wing 8.6m wide extending out 6.6m was then added to the northern half of the west side. This part still contains a stair and an entrance doorway on the south side with an ancient yett. On the wing NW corner and the main block SE corner are sets of five pyramidal corbels for square bartizans. The castle was occupied by the MacCarthys until the late 17th century. Ruined by 1750, it was restored by the Hodder family and has recently been renovated again.

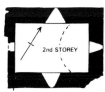

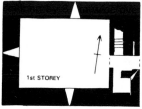

Plans of Aghamarta Castle   *Ballinacarriga: plan*

BALLINACARRIGA   W287508   B

Set on a rock is a tower measuring 14.6m by 11.8m with a short section of a bawn wall adjoining the NE corner, and part of a round flanker to the east. There is a sheila-na-gig over the east facing doorway, which has been rebuilt but retains a portcullis groove and has corbels for a machicolation above. It admits to a lobby with a guard room adjoining to the south and a spiral stair in the NE corner. Above the lobby are six levels of subsidiary chambers, the lowest two being reached from the second and third storey main chambers. The third storey is a vaulted loft and there are bartizans on the NW and SE corners at this level. In the south wall are fireplaces at the second and fourth storeys. The window embrasures at these levels have carvings, those on the fourth storey including the Instruments of the Passion, figures thought to be St John, St Mary and St Paul, and the date 1585 with initials of Randal Muirhily (Hurley) and Catherine O'Cullane. The figure accompanied by five rosettes on the second storey is thought to represent Catherine and her five children. After the Hurleys were forfeited in 1654 the castle went to the Crofts.

BALLINCOLLIG   W587698   G

The northern half of the bawn was probably built by the Barretts after their purchase of land here in 1458. So the tall tower measuring 5.8m by 4.8m now lying isolated near the east side originally lay near the east end of the south wall (now only represented by foundations), probably with a gateway beside it. The tower has four storeys, all vaulted except the topmost level with modern windows, spiral stairs linking the three upper levels. The date 1857 and the W commemorate repairs by the Wyse family. A hall lay on the north side of the bawn, where there are two single ogival-headed windows (under ivy) and a third window of two lights further east, beyond which was a corner tower containing a latrine. On the west are steps to the wall-walk and remains of a latrine. In the 16th century the bawn was extended southwards to occupy the rest of the rock outcrop, resulting in an irregularly shaped single enclosure 56m long by up to 34m wide. Here the wall contains gunloops and there is a latrine recess on the south side. Within the SE corner is a tower 5m wide containing three levels under a vault which has survived the collapse of the outer wall of a straight stair in the north wall leading up from the second storey.

During a squabble over possession in 1591 Andrew and William Barrett broke into the castle and expelled Edmund Barrett. The castle was sold to Sir Walter Coppinger in 1630 after being mortgaged to him by the Barratts for several years. It changed hands three times during the wars of 1641-52 and was captured by Williamite forces in October 1689.

Ballincollig Castle

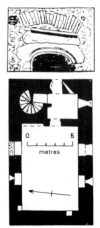

Ballinoroher: plan & view

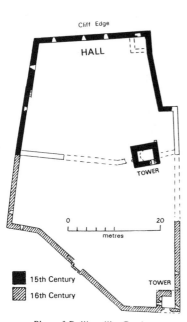

Plan of Ballincollig Castle

Cliff Edge

HALL

TOWER

0   20
metres

■ 15th Century

▨ 16th Century

TOWER

Ballynacarriga Castle

BALLINGUILE R541120

The west end wall of a tower measuring 9.3m by 7.2m stands four storeys high but has a gap from ground level to gable as result of the sills and lintels of inserted brick windows having gone. The entrance must have been in the east wall and there was probably a spiral stair in the SE corner, where there is now a range extending south to and end wall with two levels of fireplaces. Footings suggest a wing was added on the north side of the tower. The tower belonged to the Stapletons but passed in the 17th century to the Percivals, and then to the Freemans.

BALLINOROHER W425445

First mentioned in 1611, when probably fairly newly built, this castle of the Sliocht Inghine Ui Chruimin sept of the MacCarthys guarded a ford of the Argideen River. Measuring 15.5m by 9m, it has chimney stacks serving fireplaces in the lowest two levels in the north wall and a fourth storey fireplace in the south wall. There are four levels of smaller rooms over the segmental-arched entrance in the east wall, all except the uppermost being reached off the spiral stair in the NE corner. The hoodmoulded upper windows are of two or three lights, some with ogival heads, and some with gunloops on either side.

BALLINTERRY W820904

Since the 1840s most of the walls of a bawn 50m square around a late 17th century L-plan house have either gone or been rebuilt. Of four circular flankers 5.5m in diameter only that at the NE corner now survives, with six gunloops and a rebuilt upper level.

Ballinvard Castle

Ballyannan Castle

Ballycrenane: plan

BALLINTOTIS   W932729

The west wall of this tower measuring 7m by 6.2m contains a stair from a blocked entrance to a spiral stair in the SW corner. Yet another stair leads to the NW corner of the fourth storey, which has three windows, a latrine and another stair to a still complete wall-walk and parapet. A bell was mounted in a south merlon. The vaulted third storey can only have been reached by a hatch from below. The tower was granted to George Moore in 1579 but was soon recovered by the FitzGeralds.

Ballybeg: plan

BALLINVARD or ROSSMORE   W312471

This late 16th century four storey O'Hurley tower on a rock plateau was forfeited in the 1650s and later granted to the Archbishop of Dublin. The east wall contains the entrance lobby with a guardroom on one side and a spiral stair in the SE corner. Above the lobby are chambers with fireplaces, and in the partition wall there are also fireplaces serving the main chambers, with a chimney stack on top. Many of the window embrasures are fitted with gunloops. There are square bartizans on the NE and SW corners and a box-machicolation over the entrance doorway.

Ballintotis: plan

BALLYANNAN   W867714

Sir John Broderick built this Scottish-style house in the 1650s probably from the materials of a Hodnett tower. Of two storeys and an attic, it measures 15.6m by 6.5m over walls 0.75m thick and has circular towers 5.2m in diameter at the SW and NE corners. The towers both have chimney stacks serving two levels of fireplaces and the main block had similar stacks at each end, although the northern one has fallen. There were large windows at ground level and although the plan would allow flanking fire the house has no gunloops or machicolations. Outbuildings continue the line of the main block northwards and there is a slightly later square staircase wing in the middle of the west side, where the ground level is higher. A new house was built further east in the 18th century.

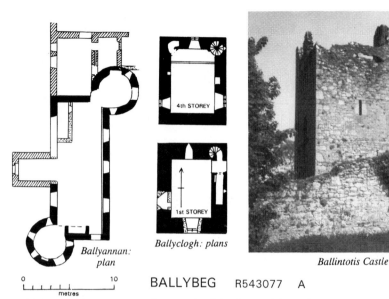

Ballyannan: plan

Ballyclogh: plans

Ballintotis Castle

Ballinvard: plan

BALLYBEG   R543077   A

Just north of the Augustinian priory lies the vaulted basement of a tower measuring 8.8m by 7m with an entrance facing west and three double-splayed loops. The lost upper levels had a latrine in the NE corner and must have had a separate entrance since there is no stair. A more complete tower containing two storeys under a vault and two more above lies by the NW corner of the claustral buildings. The upper levels are linked by a spiral stair and have mural chambers over the east facing entrance.

BALLYCLOGH   R493021

This castle of the MacRoberts branch of the Barrys was forfeited in 1641 and given to the Purdons. In the early 19th century the tower measuring 9.2m by 8m in the SE corner of a 30m square bawn was adapted as a residence for the estate steward and the bawn filled with lean-to buildings, all now derelict. The tower lowest storey has a double-splayed loop and is vaulted with a hatch at the SW corner and has a doorway facing north. A set of 19th century steps lead to an upper door into a spiral stair rising at the NE corner from the second storey to the fourth storey, and then a straight stair in the north wall leads to the fifth storey. The second storey has a latrine in the east wall. The third storey has a vault and contains the only original fireplace (with a 19th century one inserted) although there are chimney stacks on all four sides. There are square bartizans on pyramidal corbels at the NE and SW corners but the main parapet has gone and the roof is collapsing.

BALLYCRENANE   X022688

This tower of the Imokilly FitzGeralds was damaged in 1642, but was restored and remained occupied by the Tyntes and their successors the Wallises until damaged in 1798 by a bombardment from a ship which had been refused supplies. The upper parts were dismantled in 1885, leaving just a ground floor room with rebuilt north and south walls and the lower parts of a second storey loft under a former vault. The west wall contains a doorway with a portcullis slot and a stair leading up southwards.

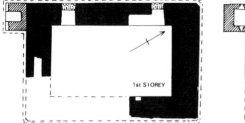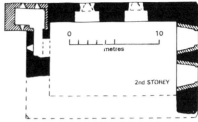

Plans of Ballyderown Castle

BALLYDEROWN   R847007

Set beside an agricultural institute on a cliff above the Araglin river is a hall house measuring 19m long by 12.4m wide over chamfered-cornered walls 2.3m thick above a battered base. It is thought to have been built by the Condons c1200-20 although the first mention of it occurs shortly after David Condon's murder in 1342. An added 3m wide turret projecting south at the SW corner contains latrines on two upper levels with an intermediate level that can only have been reached by a trapdoor. A stair in the south end wall connected the main hall with the dark cellar below it. Probably there was an upper doorway at the south end of the east wall, which has now fallen. The hall had two windows in the west wall and another two in the north end wall, the latter being insertions of c1600 with mullions and transoms, now destroyed apart from a fragment of a hoodmould. One west window remains of a third storey which was probably created later within the original roof space.

BALLYHANDLE   W552615

A platform 40m by 35m above a drop to a stream is enclosed by a ditch 8m wide on the west, north and east, with a causeway at the NW corner. Inside is the very ruined lowest part of a Barry Oge tower measuring 8m by 6m with traces of three double-splayed loops and a vaulted loft above. A length of thin walling runs north from the NE corner.

Ballymacphilip Castle

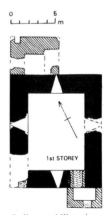

Ballymacphilip: plan

Ballyderown Castle

Ballyhooly Castle

BALLYHOOLY   W728989

Beside a 19th century house above the north side of the Blackwater is a tower measuring 9.7m by 7.5m plus parts of the north and west walls of a bawn with a two storey NW corner flanker 5.5m in diameter with a dome vault and gunloops. The tower is entered through a three storey addition at the east end, the pointed-headed doorway being commanded by a box-machicolation from the level above. The annex contains timber stairs leading to the foot of a spiral stair in a turret at the NE corner. This turret has two levels of vaulted rooms above the modern roof and parapets and a bellcote on its NW corner. The vaulted second storey with an inserted oculus loop, and the third storey each have fireplaces in the west end wall. The fourth storey has another vault, a piscina by the SE corner, and a fireplace in the south wall inscribed "M.L. restored 1862". The fifth storey has a blocked fireplace at the east end. These top two levels have mullion-and-transom windows, of two lights except for one of three on the north side.

BALLYMACPHILIP   R740969   Early tower with two wings. Now farm store

This three storey building measuring 12m by 10.2m has remains of an added four storey turret projecting from the east end of the south end wall, and a wing 5.4m by 4m above a battered base added to the west end of the north wall. A gap at the SW corner represents where there was a spiral stair rising from an entrance doorway with a portcullis groove. The second storey was a vaulted loft reached only by a timber stair or ladder from below. The third storey has arcading on corbels on all sides except the south. There are pointed-headed windows made without cut stone, the central one of three in the east wall being wider and segmental-headed. The NW wing contained a spiral stair linking the uppermost of five levels of rooms, all once vaulted, the second and fifth having latrines. The castle was granted to Arthur Hyde in 1588 but remained in Roche hands until 1611.

Bawn flanker at Ballymaloe   *Ballynamona Castle*

BALLYMACSHANROE   W836694

A Barry tower measuring just 6.8m by 5.4m now covered by a corrugated iron roof and having a modern parapet lies in the yard of Ashgrove House on the north shore of Great Island. It has two levels below a vault and a top storey with a window on each side, a later fireplace in the west wall. The staircase projects into the upper room.

BALLYMALOE   W953679   H

The two storey high and six bay wide entrance front of the house now used as a restaurant and guesthouse was built c1820 to replace most of the original tower probably built by Richard FitzMaurice FitzGerald, a son of the Knight of Kerry who was made seneschal or governor of this district by the Earl of Desmond in 1440. Richard's descendants were the FitzGeralds of Imokilly. Still surviving at the west end is a small added turret with a modern parapet containing several small vaulted rooms. Added to the tower north wall and rising from a lower level is a four storey mid 18th century block added by Hugh Lumley. Reset upon this part is a plaque dated 1602 with initials and arms of John FitzEdmund FitzGibbon. Adjoining the house SE corner is an L-plan block probably of the 1660s, recently restored and re-roofed. From the house east wall a 10m length of the 5m high bawn wall leads out to the 4.4m square NE corner flanker of the bawn, with gunloops on two levels. The gateway beside the tower has an arch dated 1709 but the original arch is said to have been dated 1603. South of it lie 19th century farm buildings and coach houses. The castle passed to Lord Broghill after the rebellion of 1641-2 and in 1672 he retired to Ballymaloe, before transferring later to Castlemartyr.

BALLYNAMONA R651075 D

The Nagles built this tower probably c1600, occupying it until the 19th century, when a house, now demolished, was built against the tower north wall. It measures 11.6m by 8.2m and has an entrance in the east wall, with a stair rising to where a spiral stair begins at the SE corner. None of the four main chambers is vaulted. The third storey has windows with pairs of ogival-headed lights on each side near the west end. At this level each side has a gable-shaped recess with a gunloop in the apex from a mural chamber. There is a box machicolation from the top storey over the entrance, and the NE and SW corners have bartizans. There is a blocked angled gunloop opening from a chamber in the east wall at second storey level. A sheila-na-gig formerly on the tower has been lost.

BALLYROBERTS W880928

In a modern farmyard stand two four storey high fragments of a 15th century Barry tower about 9m square but with a step in the now-destroyed middle part of the north wall. The east wall contains several double-splayed loops, and there is another facing north in the NW corner fragment. There are traces of a third storey vault.

BALLYVODOCK W854705

This Hodnett tower near the shore later passed to the O'Cahills and is said to have been blown up in the 1640s. Only the 5m high SE corner stands higher than the lowest storey and the walls are very defaced. The south wall contained a doorway at the west end and the other three walls each had a central loop.

Ballyvodock: plan

BANDON W492551 C

Fragments remain of the walls built by Richard Boyle, Earl of Cork between 1620 and 1627, especially a low section with a parapet on either side of a wall-walk running south of the river on the west side. The walls were dismantled in the 1690s and nothing remains of the main east and west gates of the southern part, or of the north gate of the part north of the river, although they lasted into the 18th century.

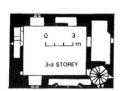

3rd STOREY

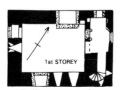

1st STOREY

Ballynamona: plans

Ballyvodock Castle

Barnahely Castle

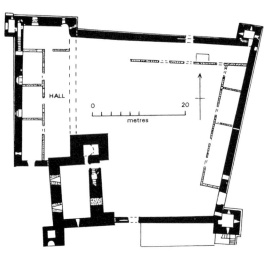

Plan of Barryscourt Castle

BARNAHELY   W 773637   C

Remains of a house of 1796 called Castle Warren lie on the east side of a bawn about 30m square, and farm buildings extend from it along the north side. A late 16th or early 17th century range 20m long by 9m wide occupies the bawn SE corner. It has a large kitchen fireplace with an oven at the east end. The upper level has a large fireplace with a shallow breast facing the court and a smaller fireplace with a corbelled lintel further east in the south wall. Five pyramidal corbels support a slab-roofed bartizan on the SE corner. The SW corner has a doorway out onto the 15m length of bawn wall-walk to the west. Below this section is a gunloop. Just north of the now destroyed SW corner of the bawn is the oldest part of the complex, a much altered tower 7.2m wide by 10.5m long now containing just one upper room over a vaulted cellar, probably built c1530 by Richard de Cogan. His descendants lived here until in 1642 a garrison of 40 men surrendered to Lord Inchiquin after a short bombardment. A thousand barrels of wheat were then found within the castle. It later passed to Judge John Cooke, whom Charles II had hanged as a traitor in 1660, suitable retribution for a man who had condemned many royalists. What was described as a "defaced mailed head" once upon the walls was sold off c1925.

Barryscourt Castle

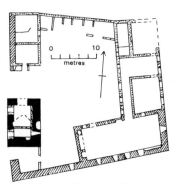

Plan of Barnahely Castle

BARRYSCOURT   W822725   E

The Barrys had their chief seat here until they transferred to Castle Lyons after the death of David Barry in 1617. He had rebuilt the tower at Barryscourt damaged during the rebellion of 1581, after which it was briefly occupied by Sir Walter Raleigh. David's son, another David, transferred his main seat to Castle Lyons after he was created Earl of Barrymore in 1627. Lord Inchiquin captured Barryscourt in May 1645. It later passed to Stephen Coppenger, who built a new house beside the castle in 1716.

The castle has an irregularly-shaped bawn about 34m wide extending 30m to the east of the now-vanished inner east wall of a hall block occupying much of the west side. The hall itself retains two windows of two lights with seats in the embrasures in the battered west wall which may be 13th or 14th century work set upon still earlier foundations. The hall was about 26m long by 10m wide internally, although the north end, projecting beyond the 15th century bawn wall, may have been divided off as a private chamber. This end has a stair in the west wall and access to latrines in a west facing turret on the NW corner. The 1.5m thick bawn walls rise 4m to the wall-walk and are flanked by a north-facing turret 4.5m square at the NE corner and a similar turret which clasps the SE corner. The NE turret has a vaulted upper room with gunloops. There is a gateway immediately north of the SE turret, and there is another entrance with a pointed arch and drawbar slot in the north wall. Ruined ranges of 19th century farm buildings now abut the north and east sides of the bawn, and also occupy the interior of the former hall block. A still-roofed building lies along the outside of the bawn south wall.

Extending from the hall block SE corner is a tower house 15m long by 10.4m wide containing a cellar with restored double-splayed loops, a lower hall given a barrel-vault to replace the original pointed vault in the rebuilding of the 1580s, and an upper hall. A chamber set in the east haunch of the vault and reached from the upper hall has been mostly filled in. A wing 7.8m by 5.6m clasping the NE corner contains five storeys of rooms, the second and third levels being reached from the lower hall, and the fourth storey chapel and the private room above it (with a latrine) being reached from the upper hall. An added turret 4m square projects boldly from the SW corner. Its second level has a latrine for the lower hall. Four upper levels, the lowest with a very low doorway and the next having a latrine, are all reached from the upper hall via an ogival-headed doorway onto a spiral staircase. A turret 2.5m wide projecting 1.7m from the south end of the east wall contains six levels of even smaller rooms. The 2.4m thick east wall of the main block contains a stair rising from the entrance beside the NE wing to doorways into the two halls. The entrance is protected by a gunloop off the stair and by a murder hole from a small room above. Originally there may have been an entrance higher up further south. The lower hall is dimly lighted by a loop facing south and loops either side of a fireplace on the west. Each of the east and west sides of the upper hall originally contained a central two-light window and a three-light window closer to the north end, but the western central window was blocked by an inserted fireplace dated 1588 and the flue of the lower hall fireplace, probably also of that period. There was also a window at the south end.

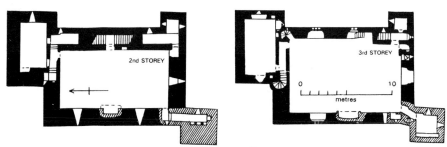

Plans of tower house at Barryscourt

Black Castle

Barryscourt Castle

BELVELLY   W792706   C

The Hodnets built this tower measuring 13.5m by 10m in the 15th century to guard a ford onto Great Island replaced by a bridge in 1807. Sir Walter Raleigh tried to obtain a grant of it in 1581, describing the tower as "broken down" to minimise its value. It was occupied by Sir Peter Courthorpe for a rent of £60 a year throughout the Civil War period. The worn plaque over the entrance doorway near the south end of the north wall probably depicted his arms. The entrance lobby is covered by a large murder hole from the lowest of a tier of four mural chambers connected by a spiral stair in the SW corner. This stair also connects three upper main rooms above a vaulted loft reached by a stair from the cellar NE corner. The upper rooms each have a slop-stones in the SW corner and centrally placed windows facing east, south and north, those of the topmost room being of two ogival-headed lights (now lacking mullions), some with sunken spandrels externally. The third storey has a chamber in the SE corner and the chamber in the west wall has a latrine in the NW corner. A stair from the topmost window embrasure on the south leads up to an extra room, now much ruined, upon the west gable, and to a wall-walk now lacking a parapet upon the south wall. In the 1920s the Irish army replaced some of the lower window loops with concrete horizontal slits to make the tower useable as a blockhouse.

BENDUFF or CASTLE SALEM   W269386

The Annals of the Four Masters records the building of this tower by Catherine MacCarthy Riabhach (nee FitzGerald), d1506. In the 1660s William Morris removed the top and put a slate roof over the third storey, which has a fireplace on the north and an ogival-headed window facing west, with a similar window below it. The tower east wall contains passages and chambers, the blocked entrance, and the spiral stair in the SE corner, with latrines in the NE corner. Beyond is a modernised late 17th century house, known as Castle Salem, built by William's son Fortunatus. It has a chimney stack corbelled out at second storey level on the north side. A terraced garden lies to the east.

BLACK CASTLE   V869278   D

A concrete bridge leads to a promontory by Toormore Bay on which stands a O'Mahony tower measuring 11.9m by 8.8m, also known as Leamcon. It was surrendered to Captain Roger Harvey in 1602 after he brought up a "sow" to breach the landward wall, and was burnt in 1641 to prevent the O'Mohonys from using it. The tower has recently been modernised as a summer residence. One north window is ogival-headed. The lowest two levels each have entrances in the east wall and a stair leads southwards from the upper entrance to a third storey over a vault. There is a latrine chute in the north wall.

BLACKROCK   W724720   H

Surmounted by a gothick tower of 1828-8, with further buildings and a court of that date at the back, are the two lowest levels of a circular four storey tower built c1582 on the north bank of the River Lee by the citizens of Cork to guard this approach to the city. In the 18th and 19th centuries the castle was used by the city corporation for functions. The tower is 10.4m in diameter over walls 2.2m thick and has blocked double-splayed loops for cannon in the lowest level, which is reached by a spiral stair. The second level now forms part of a restaurant and now has wooden-framed windows inserted into the gunports. In the foyer, reset upon the outside wall of the original tower, is a fireplace transferred here from Ronayn's Court with an IHS monogram, shields, fleur-de-lis, a Tudor rose, and the inscription "Morris Ronayn and Margaret Gould builded this house in yeare of oure lorde 1627 and in the 3 yeare of Kinge Charles. Love God and neighbors".

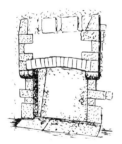

*Fireplace at
Barryscourt*

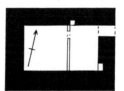

Black Castle: plan

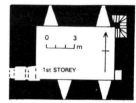

Belvelly: plan

Belvelly Castle

Blarney Castle

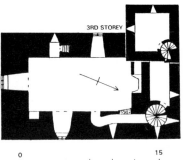

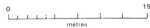

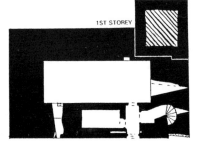

Blarney Castle

Plans of Blarney Castle

BLARNEY   W608753   E

This huge tower on a rock near the confluence of the Martin and Blarney rivers is said to have once borne a stone with the date 1446 and the name of Cormac Laidir MacCarthy, who lived until 1494. He may not have obtained the site before the 1480s and in any case date stones do not normally occur so early, so this one was probably added during a remodelling by Donal MacCarthy in the 1590s. Donal was noted for his ability to procrastinate and talk himself out of trouble, professing to be loyal to Queen Elizabeth but actually doing whatever he wanted. This is the origin of the gift of eloquence associated with the famous Blarney stone, which is one of the central southern lintels of a series carrying a new double-stepped machicolated parapet of that period across a series of tall pyramidal corbels around the east, south and west sides. The stub of the original parapet now forms a step in the wall-walk 22.5m above the ground outside. The castle was captured by Lord Broghill in 1646 and again by Cromwell in 1649, when the garrison are said to have escaped through a tunnel in the cliff below the north end of the tower. Donagh, 4th Earl of Clancarty lost his estates after James II's defeat and in 1701 Blarney was purchased by Sir James Jefferys, later Governor of Cork. He added a new east block rising up from a lower level, abandoned by a descendant for a new house nearby in 1874.

The oldest part is the slightly lower wing projecting from the north end of the west wall. It has a bartizan of the 1590s on the SW corner but was originally a self contained 15th century tower 6.8m by 5.6m with four rooms connected by a spiral stair in the NE corner. The lowest room (the base is solid or a long-forgotten chamber has been filled in) has a vault and a later oriel window opening out above the cliff edge to the north, and is at about the same level as the second of the five storeys of the later main block probably added in the early 16th century. The second storey of the wing has a corner loop facing SW. The third storey is vaulted and the presence of a solid floor allowed the conversion of the fourth storey into a kitchen with fireplaces in the west and south walls.

Oriel window at Blarney

Gateway at Blarney

The main block measures 19.4m by 11.4m and is entered from a terrace on the east side by a pointed-arched doorway with a drawbar slot. The wall is here 3.7m thick and contains a mural chamber opening off the entrance lobby, from which rises a spiral stair in the NE corner. A loop beyond the chamber has an inserted gunloop towards the terrace gateway to the SE. There is also a loop in the north wall, here 4.1m thick, but higher up thickened to 5.3m to contain a passage linking the two staircases at second storey level, a latrine above, then a chamber at third storey level, and then another latrine, reached by a winding passage like that below. There is no separate mural chamber at the top for the fifth storey main room extends the full length of the building. Above the pointed vault over the second storey the other walls reduce in thickness and at the top the west wall is only 1.6m thick. In the 1590s mullioned windows of two and three lights were inserted into the three upper levels, but the top north window retains two original ogival-headed lights.

The gateway at the south end of the east terrace has a semi-circular arch with a dropped keystone with a hoodmould over and lies in a block 16m long by 4m wide with a vaulted upper room. The 18th century range rising from below the terrace is built with corbelling over the lower two storeys of an earlier U-shaped turret at the north end, and there is evidence of a second turret closer to the main tower. On the west side of the original tower the north wall of a bawn with gunloops in the merlons continues along the cliff edge after a gap of 14m and ends in a round flanker about 5m in diameter with gunloops on two levels. Two other flankers lie some distance to the south, that to the SE being 9m in diameter and adjoining a later stable block, whilst the SW flanker was no more than a small turret set on a rock outcrop. At about 200m by 70m the bawn thus enclosed would have been too large to easily defend and may have been subdivided.

BRYAN'S FORT   W188314

Above the south side of Castle Haven Bay is a small square court with corner flankers furnished with gunloops, those on the NW and SE being very ruined. The northern flankers had two levels. The southern flankers were mounts with gunports for cannon commanding the bay and are solid at court level. Part of a wall-walk remains between them. An upper fireplace and gable survive on the east side. The fort was built c1650 by Colonel Richard Townsend and saw considerable military action in 1690.

Buttevant Castle

Buttevant: plans

BUTTEVANT   R543086   C

A castle here is first mentioned in 1364, when the Barrys held it as tenants here of the bishop of Lismore, but it may have existed by 1234, when David Barry was allowed to hold a fair and market at Buttevant. The castle was captured by Lord Deputy Sir Henry Sidney in 1568. It was ruined by 1750 but was later purchased and rebuilt by the provisions merchant John Anderson. It then passed in turn through a succession of families. The southern part of the complex of ruins on a cliff above the west side of the Awbeg river appears to represent a 13th century courtyard castle about 25m across. Of it there remain parts of the east, west and south walls and a much altered tower 10m in diameter at the SW corner containing a lofty dome-vaulted room and two upper levels of hexagonal rooms originally with latrines in the south curtain wall. New windows and battlements were provided c1800 when a new south show front was erected with a SE bay giving the appearance of a second tower. The northern court with 19th century outbuildings but some medieval work in the east wall was probably a later addition.

BUTTEVANT   R542088   C

On the west side of the main street of the town are remains of Lombard's Castle, named after a wealthy family who may have lived in it until the 1730s, latterly as tenants of the Giffords. It was later used as a school. The remains, now two storeys high, were patched up in 1886. They comprise the south end of a main block about 19m long by 8.5m wide and a NE corner tower 5m by 4m with another section of the east wall adjoining it. Fireplaces remain in a short stump of the west wall. It appears that originally there were three other corner towers. In 1317 John de Barry was given a grant to enclose the town with walls and a north gateway is mentioned in 1375. Their exact line is uncertain.

Carrigacunna: plans

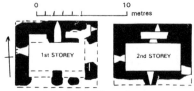

Carrigaline: plans

CAHERMONE W896742

A stone in the nearby farmyard has the date 1579 and the initials of John FitzEdmund FitzGerald, which have come from a fragmentary range with gunloops and a chimney stack over fireplaces overlooking the River Dungourney. Further south is a tower measuring 14m by 11m probably built c1450 by John FitzGerald, third son of Maurice, Knight of Kerry. A straight stair connects two levels under a vault, both with doorways facing north, and then a spiral stair leads up to a third storey with a mural room in the north wall with a latrine and murder-hole over the upper entrance. There were two more storeys, the fourth level having another vault, but little remains of them. In the 1650s the castle passed to Sir John Broderick.

CARRIGABRICK W826991

High above the east side of the Blackwater is a circular tower 11.5m in diameter probably built by Richard Condon, Sheriff of Cork, who was pardoned by the authorities for his misdemeanours in 1567. It was later forfeited and granted in 1588 to Arthur Power but was burnt by rebel Irish in the 1640s. The western portion containing a tier of mural chambers over the entrance, and any fireplaces the upper rooms once possessed, has fallen. The rest still stands five storeys high with remains of a pointed vault over the second storey and a barrel-vault over the fourth storey. Just a trace remains of a spiral stair linking the four upper levels, which all had square rooms. Only the lowest level, with three deeply splayed loops, was circular. The second storey windows are flanked by gunloops, and there are corbels for three machicolations at the top, the entrance being covered by a missing fourth one. A latrine reached off the stair is squeezed in between the second and third storeys on the north side and there is a similar arrangement above at a level between the fourth and fifth storeys.

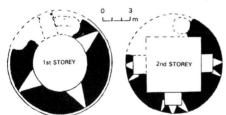

Plans of Carrigabrick Castle

Lombard's Castle at Buttevant

Carrigabrick Castle

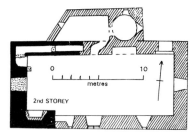

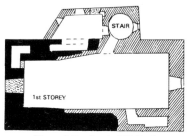

Carrigacunna Castle

Plans of Carrigadrohid Castle

CARRIGACUNNA   W663989

The Nagles held this tower above the south side of the Blackwater until Sir Richard Nagle, Attorney-General to James II, was forfeited after the king's defeat. It was then granted to the Sydneys and latter passed to the Footts. A nearby 19th century house is inhabited and the tower itself, although roofless in 1847, now has a roof, floors and battlements of 1882. Probably of mid 16th century date, it measures 11.5m by 8.6m and has in the east wall a tier of mural chambers over the entrance, including one chamber with a latrine at an intermediate level between the second and third storeys. The spiral stair in the SE corner has a T-shaped loop at second storey level, a cross-shaped loop a higher up, and a corner loop at third storey level. The third and fourth storey main rooms have later fireplaces projecting into them and plain mullioned windows of three and two lights. There are also two-light windows in the vaulted second storey. A row of joist sockets in the north wall and a blocked doorway suggest that there was once a fifth storey attic.

CARRIGADROHID   W414724   A

A bridge adjoins the east end wall with the roadway level with the second of three storeys. This end is a 16th century extension which increased the length of the 9.6m wide 15th century tower on a rock in the River Lee from about 12m to 19.5m. At third storey level the whole south side was rebuilt and the parapet has a machicolation near the east end, whilst there are two gunloops lower down. A wing added on the north side contains a well for a wide spiral staircase and three thinly walled rooms of irregular shape, the lowest having a blocked entrance doorway and what appears to be a kitchen fireplace inserted into a former latrine chute. The interior of the main building has been much patched over the years, having been occupied until the mid 18th century by the Bowens, and then in more recent times used as a handball alley. A tablet on the castle commemorates Beotius MacEgan, Bishop of Rosscarbery, who was brought a prisoner to the castle by Lord Broghill in May 1650 and summarily hanged when, instead persuading the rebel garrison of Roches to surrender, he told them to continue their resistance.

CARRIGALINE   W744627   D

This fragmentary tower measuring 9m by 7m on a rock above the Owenboy estuary may have been built by a de Cogan who married a Prendergast heiress, but in 1439 the castle was handed over to the Fitzgeralds. Lord Deputy Sidney besieged and captured the castle from James Fitzmaurice FitzGerald in 1568 and then handed it over to the St Ledgers, to whom it had previously been mortgaged. Dating probably from that period is a second building to the south, one ivy-covered wall still standing three storeys and an attic high with a chimney stack on the gable for a third storey fireplace. The main tower higher up has a stair in the north wall with a possible latrine at its foot in the NE corner. It leads past a doorway to a vaulted loft and up to the now very ruined third storey. At ground level the south wall has two arched recesses, behind which is a blocked-up external loop. Gaps in the east and west walls indicate the entrance with a drawbar slot and another former loop.

CARRIGANASS   W048566   B

A tower 9.6m wide and probably once 14m long beside the Owvane River is said to have been built by Dermot O'Sullivan, who was blown up by his own gunpowder in 1549. It was surrendered to the English in 1602 after Dunboy was taken, and was then given a surrounding bawn 40m long and up to 20m wide at the east end. Except for some rebuilt sections, the walls have gunloops and spearhead-shaped corner flankers, although the flanker at the least vulnerable SW corner is almost square in plan. The tower had segmental-shaped vaults over the second and fourth storeys and an entrance and stair in the missing east end wall. The second storey has a mural room in the north wall and passages on either side a central west window. The short stump of the south wall shows part of a mural passage at fourth storey level. The bartizans on the western corners have a straight face set across the corner and a single corbel on each side. See page 11.

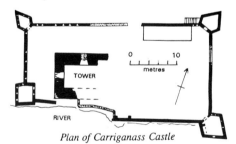

Plan of Carriganass Castle

Carrigaline Castle

Carriganass Castle

Carrigaphooca Castle

Carrignacurra Castle

CARRIGAPHOOCA   W297734 B

Dermot Mor MacCarthy is said to have built this tower on a rock above the River Sullane in 1436. Teige MacOwen MacCarthy took refuge here in 1601 after the battle of Kinsale, but it was captured and sacked by O'Sullivan Bear. The tower measures 10.7m by 9.2m and has a straight stair leading up in the east wall from the north-facing entrance to a spiral stair in the SE corner. This rises to the fifth storey and then another stair off the east window embrasure leads round the NE corner to a wall-walk with square bartizans each on five corbels at the NE and SW corners. The second and third storeys are reached off the straight stair and each have a chamber in the NW corner. The fourth storey, a vaulted loft, is reached from the stair by a lintelled passage with a latrine at the west end.

CARRIGDOWNANE   R732076

Only the south end wall about 3m high remains of a tower about 12m by 10m. Low fragments also remain of a small bawn to the west and to the north, beyond which is a sheer drop to the River Funshion. In 1317 Milo FitzPhilip de la Roche was pardoned for burning the Condon manor here, and it later passed to the Roche family. Ulick Roche was attainted in 1641 and Carrigdownane was granted in 1667 to William Harmer.

Carrigdownane Castle

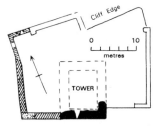

Plan of Carrigdownane Castle

CARRIGNACURRA   W239666   C

In 1602 O'Sullivan Bere captured this late 16th century tower on a rock by the River Lee which was the chief seat of the O'Learys. It was forfeited in 1641 but restored in the 1660s to the MacCarthys, the O'Learys then occupying it as tenants. In the 18th century it was obtained by the Masters family. The tower measures 11.5m by 7.6m and has a spiral stair in the NE corner rising from a destroyed east-facing entrance, over which was a room with a murder-hole and access to a small room with gunloops in a triangular spur at the SE corner. The third storey is vaulted and the fourth storey has a room with gunloops in a bartizan on the NW corner. Both these levels have fireplaces in the north wall. Above the fifth storey is an attic (with original fireplace) within the modern roof.

CARRIGNAMUCK   W481753   D

Cormac Laidir MacCarthy is said to have built this late 15th century tower now lying in the grounds of Dripsey Castle. The east wall was breached during a bombardment by Lord Broghill in 1650. The fireplaces in the north wall and the roof date from a restoration by the Bowen-Colthursts in 1866, whilst the fireplaces in the west wall at fourth and fifth storey levels are ancient if not original. The tower measures 12.8m by 9.8m and has a wing 5.2m wide projecting 3m from the north end of the east wall, beside which is the entrance doorway, with a pointed arch set in a rectangular frame. On the second storey a passage off the spiral stair in the west part of the wing gives access to a latrine east of the stair and through to the vaulted main room via a lobby with a murder hole over the entrance lobby. The third storey has another latrine tucked beside the stair. The passage to the fourth storey room contains a straight stair up to the SE corner of the fifth storey main room, from which a stair in the SW corner leads to the wall-walk, now lacking its parapet. There are fourth and fifth storey rooms in the wing, the latter originally slab-roofed, and a fireplace remains of an attic room above.

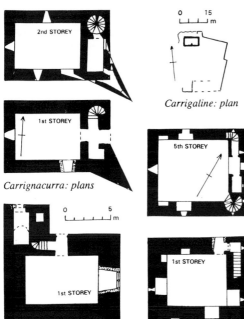

Carrignacurra: plans

Carrigaline: plan

Carrignamuck: plan   Carrigaphooca: plans

Carrignamuck Castle

Carrigrohane Castle

CARRIGNAVAR   W675815

A tower supposedly built in 1616 by Daniel MacCarthy stood two storeys high c1907, but only the west wall with a projecting turret at the north end and the top of a doorway now stands above the 4m high pile of rubble of the rest of the building. It measured 13m east-west by 8m wide. In 1650 this was the last fortress in Muskerry to surrender to Cromwell. In the 1690s Charles MacCarthy became a Protestant to retain his lands and the castle became a centre where the Gaelic traditions of music and poetry still flourished.

CARRIGROHANE   W615717   C

On a limestone cliff above the River Lee is a 17th century stronghouse of the Barrys which was wrecked in the 1640s but restored in the 1850s as a residence for the Hoare family. The windows are all new but their hoodmoulds are original, as are the string courses between the three levels, and the bartizans containing closets off the top storey. In 1989 part of the cliff west of the stronghouse collapsed onto the road and the county council then demolished the north wall (with one large embrasure) of an older adjoining building about 13m long by 10m wide. This structure, possibly a 13th century hall-house built by the de Cogans, later passed to the Roches and then to the MacCarthys. In the 16th century a square turret containing gunloops was added at the NW corner and in modern times a stair was added against the west wall to give access to the turret upper levels.

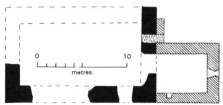

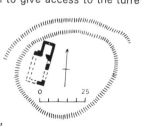

Plans of Castle Barrett

Angle-window,
Castle Barrett

CASTLE BARRETT or CASTLE MORE W560926 C

Fragments of the north and east walls of a 13th century block 16.7m by 10.1m containing a hall over a basement lie within the NW corner of an oval platform 46m by 42m with a ditch 17m wide and 2m deep. More survives of a late medieval wing 6.3m wide providing a solar block projecting a further 6.8m beyond the north wall. It has a vaulted basement and three upper storeys, two of them having fireplaces in the east wall, although the upper parts of the west and south walls have gone. The topmost room has a two-light NE window with the transom forming the corner of the block. This corner has corbels for a former bartizan. The battlements were reached by a stair rising up through the NW corner. In 1252 John de Cogan was permitted to have a weekly market and annual fair beside the castle, then known as Castle More. It was repaired during the period 1276-1281, when it was in royal hands, and was acquired by the Earl of Desmond in 1439. It only passed to the Barretts in the 17th century. They were forfeited as Jacobites in the 1690s.

CASTLE BERNARD W474544

The tower preserves a blocked entrance doorway facing north and a vault over the lowest storey. The upper levels were much altered after a two storey house was built to the east c1798, being linked to it by a corridor. The house was embattled and given turrets c1815 and has been a ruin since being burnt c1921. The tower was once known as Castle Mahon, and was the chief seat of the Kinalmeaky branch of the O'Mahonys until it was confiscated and granted in 1588 to Phane Beecher. By the 1640s it had passed to the Bernard family. They were attacked here in 1690 by a Jacobite force led by Colonel MacCarthy, and several retainers were killed.

Castle Barrett

Carrigrohane Castle

Castle Cooke

Castle Cooke

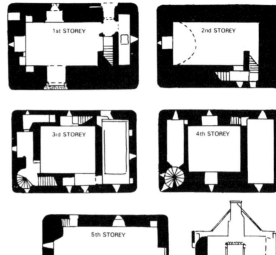

1st STOREY

2nd STOREY

3rd STOREY

4th STOREY

5th STOREY

0   5
⌐_____⌐ m

Castle Cooke: plans & section

CASTLE COOKE   R877035

Now named after its later owners, the Cookes, this was a Condon tower originally and has the round corners they seem to have preferred. Lying high above the west side of the Araglin River, it measures 14.1m by 9.1m. The defaced entrance facing the river has a drawbar slot and is covered by a machicolation off the wall-walk. At ground level the south end wall contains a guard room with a pit prison below it, so there is the unusual arrangement of a stair rising straight ahead from the entrance lobby to reach the west wall, where there is a doorway into the vaulted loft forming the second storey. Another straight stair then leads up to where a spiral stair begins in the NW corner to link the third, fourth and fifth storeys. The much ruined fifth storey room, set over another vault, is by far the largest and has a fireplace at the south end, but it lacks the fine windows one might expect in such a chamber. The third and fourth storeys have mural chambers at both the south and north ends, resulting in the central chambers being quite modest in size and almost square. The third storey northern mural room has access to a latrine in the NE corner. The third storey main room has two ogival-headed loops. From the embrasure of the eastern one a stair leads up to the fourth storey southern mural room. This room and the unvaulted room below it with a corner fireplace are quite spacious at 2.9m by 6.8m.

CASTLE DONOVAN   W113495   C

Donal O'Donovan is said to have built this tower on a rock beside the Ilen river c1560 which passed to the Evansons in the 1650s. A spiral stair in the NW corner linked four main storeys plus an attic and the series of smaller rooms over the entrance lobby south of the stair, but these latter parts and the entrance were wrecked by the collapse of the SE corner and its bartizan, now being rebuilt by a restorer. The lowest level is vaulted, and the next two levels have fireplaces on the west, whilst the top storey has a fireplace on the east and several windows with mullions and transoms. There are gunloops flanking the second storey windows. Bartizans survive on the eastern corners.

CASTLE HYDE   W781985

Now named after Arthur Hyde, to whom it was granted in 1588, but originally a Condon stronghold known as Carriganeide, this tower measuring 13.2m by 10.3m beside a later house high above the north side of the Blackwater has lost its southern half. There were five storeys with vaults over the second and fourth levels. The NE corner has a triangular spur containing a room with a fireplace and modified gunloops at second storey level and it itself flanked by a gunloop in the tower north wall. This spur is mentioned in a lease dated 1587 to John Meaghe, which also refers to a flanker on the SE corner, an iron door double chained at the entrance in the east wall (which was covered by a gunloop), and to a thatched roof. The third storey main room has a fireplace.

CASTLE INCH   W535720

This castle in the Lee Valley was demolished in 1956 before the area was flooded by the new hydro-electricity scheme. It consisted of a trapezoidal bawn surrounding a ruinous but lofty tower 12.5m long by 9m wide with a latrine turret projecting east at the NE corner and a wing projecting from the west end of the south wall. The bawn had a entrance on the west and a flanking turret near the SE corner. The tower SE corner stood four storeys high with a section of machicolated parapet on top. The adjoining part of the south wall contained a stair connecting the third and fourth storeys. The vaulted second storey was reached by a straight stair from the entrance in the north wall. It had a fireplace and oven with a flue through the wall. Dermot MacCarthy, Lord of Muskerry died here in 1570. Dermot's son Cormac was fined and briefly imprisoned in 1593 for having attacked the castle after it had been returned to its rightful owner, Kathleen Barrett, but by 1600 Dermot's mother was living within it.

CASTLE IRE   W202335

The west corner stands two storeys high and has a double-splayed NW-facing loop on the lower level. Only the half-buried base remains of the rest of this O'Donovan castle. Traces of a joint suggest a 15th century tower 10.5m long by about 8m wide later lengthened to the SE by another 5.5m. to provide a tier of extra chambers.

CASTLE LISHEN   R401194

Built into the roadside wall beside the castle is a stone from it with the FitzGerald arms. They held this tower until the 20th century, although it was originally probably a seat of the Noonan or O'Hynowen family. Lying in a farmyard, it measures 15.2m by 9.3m and is entered by a rebuilt doorway at the north wall west end. There is a mural chamber above it. A straight stair rises from the doorway to where a spiral stair begins in the NE corner. Above the second storey vault there only survives a fragment of the north wall.

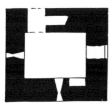

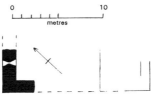

Castle Lishen: plan   *Plan of Castle Ire*   *Castle Lishen*

CASTLE LYONS   W841926   D

Castle Lyons was one of the chief seats of the Barry family by the 13th century and the southern part of the ruined mansion may partly go back to that period. Very ruined and partly covered with debris, it consists of a building with walls 1.4m thick at the SW corner with evidence of a plank-centred vault. Further east is the 4m high south wall, more than 3.2m thick, with two later openings, and part of the 2m thick west wall of a tower probably measuring about 13m by 12m. Adjoining the SE corner is the stub of a large projecting bay which formed the south end of the 8m wide east range of the mansion developed around a court about 17m square to the north after the young Lord Barrymore's marriage to Alice Boyle, daughter of the Earl of Cork, and his transfer here from Barryscourt. The northern part of the range, with walls 1.4m thick, adjoins a 6.5m wide NE range with walls of similar thickness, fragments of which still stand high enough to indicate four full storeys and an attic within the roof. In the north wall several fireplaces remain, including one 3m wide and 1.3m deep with a projecting breast. West of it the range is continued by a more thinly walled later 17th century block containing a vast kitchen fireplace backing onto the crosswall between the two ranges. These ranges are flanked on the north by a terrace 54m long and 7m wide rising 4m above the ground beyond. This part, and the west wall of an outer bawn to the south may date from the 1640s when the mansion became an important English stronghold against the rebel Irish and the headquarters of Sir Charles Vavasour. After the latter's defeat at Manning Ford Castle Lyons was captured by Lord Castlehaven. The castle remained habitable until in 1771 it was destroyed by an accidental fire caused by careless workmen leaving a soldering iron against some woodwork at the top of the building, although by that time the earls of Barrymore rarely used it as a residence.

CASTLE MACAULIFFE   R305054

All that remains of the principal seat of the MacAuliffes is a small overgrown platform with a steep slope down to the Dalua River on the east and a ditch up to 3m deep and 25m wide on the other three sides. Only a rubble mound remains of a tower on the west side.

Castle Magner

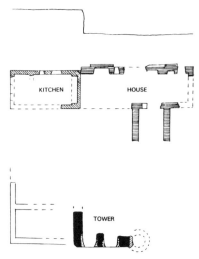

Plan of Castle Lyons

Castle Magner: plan

Castle Lyons

CASTLE MAGNER   R443019

This building is named after the Magners, who were tenants of the Barrys. They were forfeited in 1588, restored in 1618, and then replaced in the 1650s by the Bretridges. West of the glen of the Ketragh river is a fragmentary bawn, now an abandoned farmyard. A 20m length of the north side of the bawn and the return wall on the east survive, having had a two storey 18th century house built against them, now replaced by a farm building. Other fragments of the bawn wall lie in farm buildings at the NW and SW corners. Much of the four storey tower in the middle is now just a pile of rubble, but there is a fragment of the south wall with jambs of window embrasures, and a semi-circular east-facing SE corner stair turret still retains a machicolated parapet.

Castlemartyr

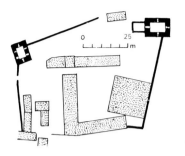
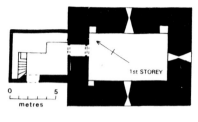

1st STOREY

Castlemartyr: plans

CASTLEMARTYR   W958731

In 1420 the Earl of Ormond, Lord Lieutenant of Ireland made James, Earl of Ormond governor of the district of Imokilly, and the latter appointed Richard, second son of his kinsman Maurice, Knight of Kerry, as his seneschal of the area. Castlemartyr was built to serve as the seneschals' seat. It was captured by Sir Henry Sidney in 1569, being abandoned by the garrison during the night after an exchange of cannonfire. It was later granted to Sir Walter Raleigh but recovered by the then seneschal, John FitzEdmund FitzGerald, only to be attacked again in 1579 by the Earl of Ormond, who hanged John's mother outside the walls. John submitted in 1583 and died in Dublin Castle in 1589. In the wars of the 1640s the castle was captured by Lord Inchiquin but then fell to a raiding party led by Sir Percy Smith. He burnt the castle and this prevented Lord Castlehaven using it as he intended as a base for the Confederate Irish forces. The castle was repaired in the 1650s and inhabited by Lord Broghill, later Earl of Orrery, until his death in 1679. It was finally abandoned after being captured by the Irish and then retaken by the Williamites in 1690, being badly damaged in the process. In the 18th century the bawn became a farmyard and coachyard serving a new house built to the west.

The castle has a bawn 65m long by 43m wide at the NW end and 50m long at the SE end, where there was a large two storey 17th century range, the inner wall of which is now missing. The outer wall has three cross-gables surmounted by tall chimney stacks serving fireplaces at ground level with flanking ovens. The west wall is continued up as a flat-topped platform reached by a stair in a polygonal turret. Just east of here are two blocked windows with mullions and transoms and hoodmoulds.

At the east corner of the bawn is a 15th century tower house measuring 13.2m by 10.4m over walls up to 2.7m thick in the vaulted lowest storey, where three sides have centrally placed double-splayed loops. The fourth side, facing NW, has upper and lower doorways protected by a small forecourt built against the bawn wall. The lower doorway has a drawbar slot and a murder hole. The upper doorway flanked by gunloops gives access to a stair up to a spiral stair in the west corner. The main third storey room has ogival-headed loops in the two end walls. The fourth storey has an inserted fireplace on the SW side, the chimney of which obstructs the SW wall-walk. There was also a window on the NE, and windows of two ogival-headed lights remain in the end walls, that on the NW having rebates for shutters, and access to a straight stair up to the fifth storey, from where a spiral stair in the west corner led to a wall-walk on the NW and SW sides, where stepped parapets still remain. The top room has lost its NE side but retains a three-light window (without mullions) at the SE end and there is also a latrine near the west corner.

At the north corner of the bawn is a second tower measuring 12m by 9m, now much altered but retaining over the second of three storeys a vault with a blocked hatch in the east corner. The lowest level has doorways opposite each other at the SW end and four loops, one in the SW having been later been converted into a fireplace. There is a ruined mural chamber in the north corner. The top room is now reached by an external stair and has an inserted fireplace in the SW end wall, and a NE end wall window embrasure with access to a latrine. A stair in the west corner rises to the wall-walk.

CASTLE MORE   W444669 G

This castle, also called Dundrinan, was one of the chief MacCarthy seats in Muskerry, having probably been built soon after they obtained this district in the mid 15th century. By the late 16th century it was held for them by the MacSweeneys and was no longer as important as their seats at Blarney and Carrignamuck. In the later 17th century it was occupied by John Bayley, and then passed to the Rye family and then the Travers family, one of whom built the L-plan 18th century house whose overgrown ruins occupy most of the west end of a bawn 45m long from east to west by 20m wide. The north side has a wall 2m thick containing a chamber high up at the west end and a blocked doorway just west of where the wall reduces to 1m thick and has footings of a building against it. On the south side there is also a length of 2m thick bawn wall adjoining a tower measuring 6.2m by 5m in the SE corner. A stair in the tower north wall leads to a spiral stair in the NE corner to all the upper levels and a wall-walk which is obstructed on the north side by the chimney stack of a fireplace on the fourth storey. The second storey has two gunloops facing south, and the third storey is vaulted. The bawn entrance lay close to the tower NE corner, beyond a short stump of the east wall but the land at this end has now been quarried away into a vertical cliff. At the SW corner is four storey tower 7.3m square, the west part of which has fallen. The doorway retains a hanging eye for the pivot of a yett. The second and third storeys were vaulted. There is a chimney stack on the south side.

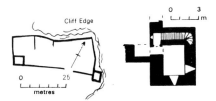

Castle More: plans

Castle More

Castlemartyr

CASTLE POOK   R615114   D

After the forfeiture of the Synan family in 1639, this tower on a rock was granted to the St Leger family, although by the 18th century the Morgans were in residence, perhaps as tenants. The tower measures 14m by 9.5m and lies in the NW corner of a bawn 45m from north to south by 40m, now only represented by buried foundations. The destroyed doorway in the east wall was flanked by a guard room and a stair leading to where a spiral stair began at the SE corner. The second storey is vaulted and has a mural chamber over the entrance. At third storey level the mural chamber in the east wall has a latrine and traces of an angle loop in the NE corner. The main room at this level has ogival-headed windows and another angle loop in the NW corner. Wooden steps from here gave access into the fourth storey room, which is vaulted, at which level there is another chamber with a latrine in the east wall. The fifth storey seems to have had a chamber in the south wall.

CASTLETOWN   R711114

A ruined house lies on the site of a castle of FitzGibbons family which in 1583 had "one hall and three chambers and three cellars enclosed within stone walls". It was captured by Lord Broghill in 1650, and later granted to the Fennel family.

Castle Widenham

CASTLE WIDENHAM   R685021

On a promontory above a bend of the Awbeg river is a late 17th or early 18th century house, remodelled and extended in the 1820s, and adjoining a five storey tower renovated c1970. It has two-light windows facing SW on the second and fourth storeys and an entrance on the NE side and faces towards where the cliff has a retaining wall with a latrine shaft. Further east is a turret over a stepped passage down to the base of the cliff. The Roches, lords of Fermoy had their principal seat here by the 13th century and the castle was originally called Dun Cruadha. It was bombarded by Lord Broghill in 1650 and after it fell the officers were shot although the men they commanded were released. Lady Roche was hanged two years later for having defended the castle. It was renamed after being granted to the Widenhams, and then passed to the Creaghs and the Smiths.

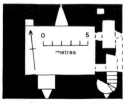

Castle Pook: plan

Clodah Castle

Cloghleagh Castle

Castle Pook

CLODAH W421654 D

This tower measuring 12.5m square is entered by a pointed-headed doorway on the west side. The lobby is flanked by a guard room and covered by a gunloop from the main room. It leads to a second lobby with access to a spiral stair in the NW corner, the steps having been renewed in 1844 by the Earl of Bandon. Part of the pointed vault over the second storey has fallen. The fourth storey has a fireplace in the east wall dated 1598 with the initials of Brian MacSweeney and his wife Orona FitzGerald. They restored the tower after it was wrecked by James FitzGerald. Of their period must also be the third storey fireplace in the west wall and the ornate upper windows have ogival heads with sunk spandrels and hoodmoulds. Some have transoms and one of three lights facing north has a wide hoodmould with horned terminals and carvings of spirals, birds, interlace, florets, fern leaf and geometrical designs. There are box-machicolations on round corbels in the middle of the south and west sides and a bartizan upon pyramidal corbels at the NE corner.

CLOGHLEAGH R827017 D

This important seat of the Condons on a cliff above the Funshion river was granted to the Fleetwoods in the 1580s, although the Condons recovered it in 1642 by managing to send in a brogue-maker who got the garrison drunk on poteen. A garrison of twenty men, eleven women and seven children surrendered to Sir Charles Vavasour in 1643 and were massacred after he left the scene. In 1684 the estate was sold to the Moores. They were created Earls of Mountcashel in 1781 and repaired the castle in the late 19th century.

The vaulted second storey of the very lofty round-cornered tower measuring 13.2m by 10.7m has access from a window embrasure to a long mural chamber in the west wall with a murder-hole over the entrance lobby. Three upper storeys are reached by a spiral stair in the NW corner. The fourth storey is also vaulted and there is a chamber in the west wall at this level. The fifth storey has an arcade on two corbels at the south end, where there is a window with two ogival-headed lights. Windows in the side walls are of just one ogival-headed light. The stair gives onto the embrasure of the north window, which was later narrowed on the east to allow the insertion of a fireplace beside it. The wall-walks and parapets on the side walls have been rebuilt. The tower lay towards the west side of a bawn about 80m square. Adjoining a fragment of the circular SW flanker about 4m in diameter is an 11m long and 3m high length of the bawn wall set on a cliff-edge.

Clonmeen Castle

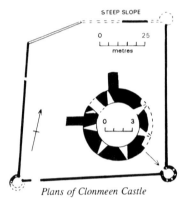

Plans of Clonmeen Castle

Remains of bishop's house at Cloyne

CLOGHPHILIP   W583761

The north and west walls of a tower measuring 12m by 10m were reduced to their footings in the 1970s. The south wall stands two storeys high, but the east wall with an inserted doorway in its base still rises through four storeys. Ivy hides the features, including inscriptions with the initials of Donogh Cormac MacCarthy with the date 1590, probably commemorating a remodelling of a structure originally erected by the Barretts.

CLONMEEN   W410989   D

A wall up to 5m high pierced with gunloops surrounds an early 17th century bawn roughly 83m square with remains of circular flankers about 6m in diameter at three of the corners, that at the SE corner being the best preserved, with several gunloops. The wall has a gap at the west end of the south side and a narrow inserted gateway near the north end of the west side. Footings of thicker walls under the bawn wall around the SE corner may be relics of an older castle here held in the 14th century by Philip O'Mol. Clonmeen was an important O'Callaghan seat until wrecked (and the clan forfeited) in the wars of the 1640s.

Coolnalong Castle

CLOYNE   W918678   C

Of the L-plan stronghouse built by John FitzEdmund FitzGerald after he took over the see demesne there remain the two storey high west wall 21m long and the 18m long north wall one storey high now part of a garden wall around the 18th century Cloyne House NE of the cathedral. Inside the house is a plaque dated 1578 with John's initials J.E.G.

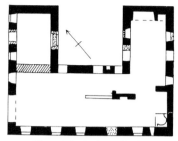

Plan of Coolnalong Castle

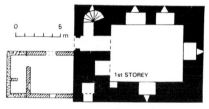

Conna: plan

Conna Castle

CONNA   W929936   B

Sir Thomas Ruadh FitzGerald, eldest son of the 14th Earl of Desmond, died in this fine tower on a rock near the River Bride in 1595. He is said to have built it c1560 (although it could be somewhat earlier in date), and it was repaired c1620 by Richard Boyle. It withstood an attack by James FitzMorris of Mocollop in 1642 but was captured by Lord Castlehaven in 1645. Although accidentally burnt in 1653, the tower seems to have been repaired and may have remained roofed until the late 19th century, when the parapet was renewed. Originally closely surrounded by a bawn, of which one 3m high fragment remains on the NW, the tower measures 13.9m by 10.2m. A box-machicolation covers the rebuilt doorway in the thick east wall, in which are mural chambers corresponding to each of the four upper storeys, all the rooms being linked by a spiral stair in the SE corner. The lowest main room has several loops in deep embrasures, including a pair facing south and one on the north later used as a fireplace. The second storey is vaulted and has a fireplace in the north wall. Most of the windows of the upper levels have ogival heads, some being of two lights. The third storey also has a fireplace and a mural chamber at this level has a latrine in the NE corner. The walls are thinner above the fourth storey vault, except on the north side, where the 5th storey room has a latrine towards the NE corner. An arch spans the east end and allows an extra mural chamber (with a fireplace) higher up.

COOLNALONG   V929421

Two wings 5.5m wide project 6.3m from the NE side of the 18m long by 7.5m wide main block of a ruined, ivy-clad stronghouse of two storeys and attics lying in a garden. One gunloop remains beside a fireplace at the south end. The building was later altered to serve as a farmhouse for Durris Court and the upper part of the SW wall has gone. The north wing became a separate dwelling and the windows were given new wooden frames. The side wall of the wings have corbels either for stone machicolations or possibly for a timber gallery. The house was probably built by Donal MacTeige MacCarthy Maclagh, who was in possession of the lands in 1631. It was granted to Colonel Reade in the 1650s and in the 1690s went to the Bernard family, later Earls of Brandon.

COPPINGER'S COURT   W260359   A

This stronghouse is named after the Cork merchant Sir Walter Coppinger, who built it during the 1620s and 30s. It lies on the south side of a thinly walled bawn 30m by 28m with traces of former outbuildings along the west side (including a SW corner oven), and has a main block 22.2m long by 8m wide over walls 1m thick. It contained offices with fireplaces at ground level, two storeys of fine state rooms with timber subdivisions between them and central lobbies, plus attic rooms for servants within the roof. Two wings 8m wide project 6.2m northwards towards the bawn and also project slightly beyond the end walls. Each wing contained four storeys of rooms (the NW wing also has a low basement) plus an attic within lengths of wall-walks with machicolated parapets upon pyramidal corbels set on the east and west walls. There are similar machicolations upon the ends of the main block south wall and on the sides of a third wing projecting from the middle of the south wall to contain a wooden scale-and-platt staircase with two attic rooms above. Gunloops cover some walls not protected by the machicolations. The lowest level of the NW wing was a kitchen with a large fireplace. Most of the windows have been ripped out, but one in the south wing still has a mullion, transom and hoodmould with stepped ends. A later Walter Coppinger and his son Dominic were both attainted by the Williamite government in 1691 since they were rebel Catholics. The house was later held by the Beecher family as tenants of the Hollow Blade Sword Company.

COPPINGERSTOWN   W903720

The SW corner of a tower about 10m wide stands four storeys high with a hen house built against it. At ground level the walls are 2.3m thick but are much reduced higher up. Only footings remain of the north wall and the east wall containing the entrance, stair, and mural chambers has gone. The second storey was vaulted and there is a latrine chute facing west. Part of a second building 8.7m wide over walls 1.2m thick and now lacking both east and west ends projects 4.5m beyond the tower west wall. It has remains of a vault and a stair on the south side. In later years this tower was held by the Coppinger family but it was probably originally built by either by the FitzGeralds or the Cotter family.

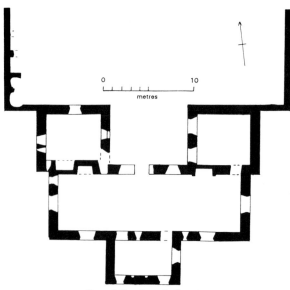

Coppingerstown Castle   *Plan of Coppinger's Court*

Coppinger's Court

CORK   W673723 & W670720

The Barrys had a tower known as Shandon Castle outside the walls close to where the Butter Market now stands north of the River Lee. A rectangular block with turrets at the NW and SE ends making a Z-plan, it is first mentioned in 1531 and was rebuilt from a ruinous state in the 1580s. The castle, then occupied by Sir George Carew's wife, was fired upon from the city walls during James I's accession to the throne in 1603 which was unpopular in Cork. Shandon castle was occupied by Cromwell during Christmas 1649, and was damaged by Williamite cannon during the siege of 1690, and had gone by 1750. The Roches are said to have had a tower, Short Castle, nearby in Shandon Castle Lane.

Excavations have revealed the lower parts of a building known as Skiddy's Castle built upon an oak raft foundation not far south of the north gate of the city. It was erected in 1445 by John Skiddy, bailiff and later mayor of Cork. During the revolt of 1603 the citizens broke into the castle, then used as a powder magazine. The upper parts were dismantled in 1785. The lower part was removed in 1892. From it has come an elaborate mantlepiece dated 1597 now set high up upon the front wall of 13 North Main Street. It bears the initials of one of the Galway family, who had by then taken possession of it.

The south island of the city was walled by 1182, and the suburb on the north island was walled during the 13th century. The area enclosed measured 650m from north to south by 220m wide and there were sixteen mural towers, a main gateway at each end and a water gate on the east side, near a tower known as the King's Castle. Another tower was known as Queen's Castle. A section of the wall on the SE side was breached during the Williamite siege of 1690. Parts of the wall remain on the south side of Hanover Street. Other fragments have been located by excavations during the 1980s and 90s.

In 1601 a detached fort was built outside the SW corner, although the existing structure here, now enclosing a police station, dates from a rebuilding of 1624. It has pentagonal bastions on the south corners, sub-rectangular bastions on the NW and NE corners, and triangular north bastion with the outermost corner rounded off.

Interior of Cornaveigh Castle

Creagh Castle

CORNAVEIGH   X052804

A tower about 10m wide and 13.5m long stands in a defaced condition upon the 15m diameter summit of a mound 7m high raised over a rock outcrop with an approach causeway on the south. A straight stair in the SW wall rises past a doorway to the vaulted second storey with a mural chamber over where the entrance lay at the foot of the stair. This FitzGerald castle is said to have been repaired by the Earl of Cork in the 17th century.

CREAGH   R619072

Close to a house of 1819 in the glen of the Awbeg river lies a Roche tower originally named Crogh (Irish for saffron - hence the townland name of Castlesaffron). It was renamed after passing to the Creagh family in the late 18th century, having passed through the hands of the Nagles, Riggs's and Loves since the 1690s. The tower measures 13.3m by 8.5m and has an entrance doorway in the SE wall. The third storey lies over an unlit vaulted loft and has an inserted fireplace and an embrasure at the NE end with an ogival headed loop and doorways off to a pair of mural chambers, one having an angle-loop in the east corner. The vaulted fourth storey has a mural chamber in the west wall. There is a latrine west corner opening off the passage from the spiral stair to the fifth storey room, which has a fireplace and two windows each with pairs of ogival-headed lights. A straight stair in the south wall then leads to the wall-walk, although this wall rises to a higher level and has a sixth storey mural chamber.

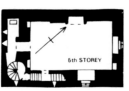
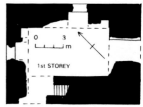

Plans of Creagh Castle

Cornaveigh: plan

Cregg Castle

Curraghoo Castle

CREGG   W769987   D

On the north side of the Blackwater is a 16th century round-cornered tower measuring 15.5m by 9.7m with a yett lying beside the entrance in the west wall, the lobby of which is commanded by a blocked cross-loop from the lowest main room. A mural chamber over the entrance has a gunloop covering it, plunging down from the sill of another loop. The main room at this second level is vaulted. The third storey main room has a fireplace, a three-light mullioned window facing north and a window of two-ogival headed lights flanked by gunloops facing south, there being access to a latrine from the west side of the embrasure. The western mural chamber at this level has ogival-headed lights with sunk spandrels. There is a second latrine in the south wall at a level between the third and fourth storeys. The fifth storey, set over a second vault, has a fireplace in the north wall and windows with pairs of ogival-headed lights set opposite each other at the east end of the north and south walls. The western mural chamber at this level has a fireplace with an oven beside it and a gutter draining through a slop stone, so it must have been a kitchen. A sixth storey mural room above with another fireplace has lost the wall between it and the attic room of the main tower. The lower parts of the parapet remain, with part of a bartizan at the NE corner and corbels for a box-machicolation over the entrance doorway. The Roches held this fine tower until they were forfeited in the 1640s.

CURRAGHHOO   R763057   D

On a rock above the Funshion River is an O'Hennessy tower measuring 8m by 6.2m which is similar to their other tower at Dunmahon. The west end wall contained separate entrances one above the other into the lowest two levels, over which there is a vault with a hatch in the NW corner. The second storey is also vaulted but little remains of the chamber above, these levels being formerly reached by a spiral stair in the now mostly destroyed SW corner.

0   3
⊢_⊥_⊣ m

Curraghoo: plan

DANNANSTOWN   R678066

Two storeys of a tower granted in 1611 to David, Lord Roche, and measuring 10.5m by 9m remain in use as a cow shed with a concreted basement and more concrete on top of the vault. The east wall contains a straight stair to the lost upper storeys. See page 90.

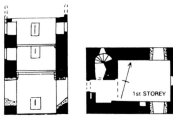

Derryleamleary: plan & section

Drishane Castle

DERRYLEAMLEARY   W364507

This three storey tower on a rock amongst marshes west of a stream belonged to the Crimeen branch of MacCarthy Riabhach. It was inhabited until the 19th century and consequently most of the openings have been remodelled with wooden frames. A bartizan on the SW corner is now hidden by ivy. The west wall contains mural rooms (one with two gunloops) set over the entrance and reached off a spiral stair in the NW corner.

DOONANORE   V946217

On the NW side of Cape Clear Island is a four storey tower measuring 8m by 7m lying on the east side of a ruinous bawn 30m by 20m with buildings in the SE corner and a D-shaped turret at the NW corner. Another enclosure to the east has remains of a building with an oven. The tower has an east entrance, from which rise flights of stairs around the very ruined SE corner, where there was a projection 2.7m wide facing south which contained a latrine higher up. The third storey has a vault of overlapping slabs carried on three pointed arches. The castle belonged to the O'Driscolls and was surrendered to Crown forces in 1602 after a short siege.

DOWNDANIEL   W758561

This tower measuring 13.5m by 9.7m at the confluence of the Brinny and Bandon rivers is said to have been built by Barry Og in 1476 but gunloops remaining in the four storey high and 1.8m thick NW wall suggest a 16th century rebuilding, when it was held by MacCarthy Reagh. There is an ogival-headed light on the third storey, which was vaulted. Of the other walls only the lower part of the SE wall remains, with a latrine chute near the south corner. The 2.5m thick SE and NE walls contained the entrance and various upper mural chambers. The castle was purchased by the East India company in 1610. It was occupied by MacCarthy Reagh in 1641 but attacked and captured by a force sent from Bandon. It later passed to the Earls of Cork.

Gateway at Dromaneen

Bawn at Dromsicane

DROMSICANE W271930

In 1750 it was claimed that this former MacDonogh MacCarthy castle had a "high square tower in the centre....lately demolished". However, the castle may actually have been founded by the O'Keeffes, and in the 1690s went to Sir Nicholas Chinnery. A bawn 41m long by 30m wide is still enclosed by a wall up to 4m high retaining three of the four circular corner flankers 7m in diameter with many gunloops. An angled loop in the east wall covered the outer part of the SE flanker. The gateway probably lay on the west side.

DUNALONG W027259

A promontory on the east side of Sherkin Island has remains of a wall isolating it, with traces of a former ditch (perhaps older) in front. North of an entrance on the site of the gateway is an internally projecting mural tower. Within the bawn lies a tower 9m by 4.8m now a farm store, having been reduced to two storeys with a floor between them and a metal roof. Both levels have doorways in the west end wall, but the lower is now blocked. From the upper doorway a passage leads south to a SW corner loop and north to a NW corner spiral stair. The north wall contains a small chamber opening off the embrasure of a loop. The citizens of Waterford attacked this castle in 1537 in revenge for the O'Driscoll owners having stolen a cargo of wine. It was garrisoned by the Spanish with fifty men in 1601. The castle was surrendered to Captain Bennett in 1645 and during the late 17th and the 18th centuries it was occupied by the Beecher family.

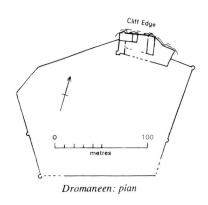

Dromaneen: pian

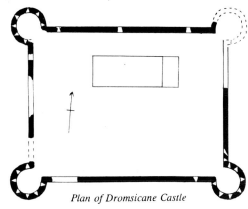

Plan of Dromsicane Castle

DUNASHAD   W047265

The level area east of this stronghouse of two storeys with attic rooms in the roof seems to have been a walled bawn. The other three sides lie on cliffs above Bartimore Harbour. Measuring 20.5m by 8m, the house was probably built in the early 17th century by the O'Driscolls on the site of an earlier fortress, but soon passed to the Coppingers until they were forfeited in the 1690s. In 1642 the O'Driscolls attempted to recover it by force.
The upper storey has segmental-arched window embrasures with roll-mouldings on the inner edge. The lights have single, double or triple ogival heads, transoms, and hoodmoulds with horned ends. There are three upper fireplaces, one at the east end having an oven on its east side. On the SW corner is a bartizan with gunloops. Some of the lower embrasures have suffered from concrete patching in the 1920s.

DUNBEACON   V903389

A three storey high and 1m thick fragment remains of the northern part of the east wall of a tower positioned on a promontory so as to close off a triangular court 15m across. There are traces of a second storey vault. Said to have been built by Donall O'Mahoney c1460, probably on the site of an older fort, it was burnt by the O'Mahoneys after the confiscations of the 1580s. The English captured the castle in 1602.

Dunbeacon Castle

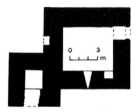

Dunmanus: plan

Dunmanus Castle

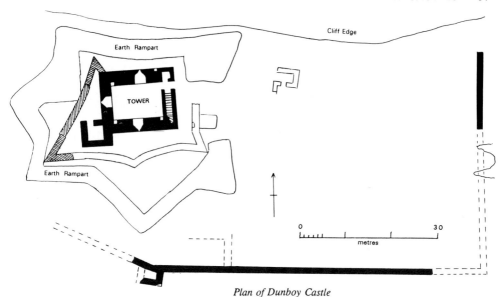

Plan of Dunboy Castle

DUNBOY   V668440

Excavations in 1967-73 around the surviving lower part of a 15th century tower built by Donal O'Sullivan Bere on a rocky promontory overlooking Bear Island Sound found footings of a wing 6.4m square at the SW corner. Also revealed were remains of a bawn wall with salient angles closely surrounding the east, south and west sides of the tower, materials for it perhaps being taken from a much larger earlier bawn 45m wide extending 65m east of the tower. This older bawn has 1m high remains of south and east walls 1.3m thick with part of a tower at an angle of the wall due south of the tower house. A cliff was adequate protection on the north side. The new inner wall is thought to have been built in the spring of 1602, when the castle was occupied by a Spanish force. It was taken by Donal Cam O'Sullivan in a night attack when a small hole was made in the wall, and then finally captured and slighted after a bombardment by a force led by Sir George Carew which caused much damage, all the garrison of 143 men eventually being executed. A new earth rampart was built just beyond this inner bawn wall when the site was refortified by the Cromwellian government in the 1650s. The tower measures 16.8m by 12.8m and has an east facing entrance with a straight stair rising from it towards the SE corner. The other three sides all have loops and there are latrine shafts on the north and west sides.

DUNDANION   W711717

Near Sir Thomas Deane's house of 1860 (now offices of Telecon Eireann) is a tower thought to have been built c1560 by the Galway family, who were prominent citizens of Cork, which lies just 3km to the west. After their forfeiture in the 1690s the tower went to two Roche brothers who mortgaged it to the Nagles. Measuring 6.6m by 5.5m, it has an entrance in the north end wall near a cliff above the flood plain of the River Lee. A straight stair then leads to a spiral stair in the NW corner to two upper storeys (neither of them vaulted) and the wall-walk. Except on the west, where the top storey has a two-light window, the windows have been modified or damaged. The second storey has a fireplace on the east and the top storey an inserted fireplace with a brick stack in the SE corner. Only the gabled north wall with a large ground level fireplace remains of a later two storey annex projecting 5.5m from the northern half of the east wall.

Dundeady Castle

DUNDEADY   W339315   D

A farmyard occupies an irregularly-shaped bawn set on the neck of Galley Head. A wall on the north side has a flanking turret with a barn backing onto it, and there is an escarpment on the south side, whilst to the east is part of a tower with two latrines chutes. NW of the farmhouse is the lower part of a tower 9m long by 5m wide with a projection 4.5m wide near the east end of the south side. The tower has a vault formed by corbelling the wall inwards and then capping with lintels. This castle belonging to Barry Roe was captured by the Irish in 1642, soon recaptured by the Parliamentarian Colonel Myn, only to be quickly reoccupied by the Barrys. Prior to the war the castle was mortgaged to the Percivals and they held it until the 19th century.

DUNLOUGH or THREE CASTLES   V730271

The lake of Dun Lough occupies half the width of the neck of a large rocky headland on the Mizen peninsular. In the 15th century the O'Mahonys built a tower 9m by 7.4m on the highest point of the other half of the neck. The tower contained a hall over two lower levels both with entrance doorways in the north wall, the hall being reached from a straight stair to its NW corner from the lower doorway. The hall floor is formed of slabs laid over two pointed arches over the second storey. Later on a wall 0.8m thick was built from the tower SW corner to the cliff-edge 22m away. A similar wall up to 6m high was built from the tower NE corner down to the lake shore 40m away. Near the lake shore is a tower 4.7m by 4.5m containing four storeys, the second having a pointed vault, and the fourth a barrel vault. A spiral stair connects the two upper levels. Beside the tower south wall is a gateway passage. At a still later period a new inner wall 1.3m thick was built to incorporate the gateway in a larger structure extending around the west and north sides of the tower. Just south of a change of alignment of the curtain wall is a central turret 3.6m wide containing tiny rooms linked by a spiral stair. The second storey has a doorway out onto the curtain wall-walk. This room and one above have vaults of overlapping slabs. The west side of the lake has remains of a wall forming a continuation of the defences. Dunlough was let to one of the Coughlans in 1627 and then was occupied by a lawless sept of the O'Donoghues as tenants of the Earl of Cork.

Dunlough Castle

DUNMAHON   R769049   D

A tower on a rock outcrop NE of the Funshion river, similar to the neighbouring O'Hennessy tower of Curraghoo, may have been built when one of that family was abbot of St Mary's Abbey at Fermoy, being listed as an abbey possession in 1541. Pardons issued to the O'Hennessys in the late 16th century describe them as of Dunmahon, although they probably held it as tenants of the Roches. On the west side the tower has separate doorways into the lower two storeys, the lowest level being vaulted. The upper doorway has steps up to a spiral stair in the SW corner. The third storey is vaulted and has a mural room on the south with access to a latrine at the east end. The fourth storey forms one large room with five window embrasures, one of which, at the west end, was later converted into a fireplace. Just one corbel remains of a former bartizan on the NW corner. There are also traces of a thinly walled bawn 50m long by 20m wide.

Dunmahon: plan

Dundeady: plan

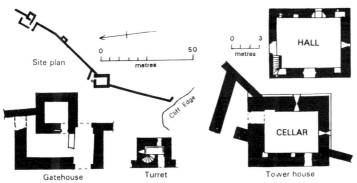

Site plan

Cliff Edge

Gatehouse

Turret

Tower house

HALL

CELLAR

Plans of Dunlough Castle

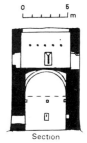

Section

DUNMANUS   V846331   D

A carved head stolen in 1972 is said to have been a likeness of Donogh More O'Mahony, who is alleged to have built this tower c1430. It was captured by Carew in 1602 but later recaptured by the O'Mahonys. They were in possession in 1641, although in the 1620s and 30s it had been occupied firstly by William Hull and then by Dermot MacCarthy Reagh. The castle was sold to Emmanuel Moore in 1655, and then sold to Sir William Petty. Of four storeys with a vault over the third level, the tower measures 9.4m by 8.6m and has a wing 5.5m square clasping the southern corner. This wing has a vaulted cellar, a room above, and then three upper chambers all reached by doorways and stairs from the SW corner of the main tower topmost room, which has windows with paired ogee-headed lights. There are separate NE-facing entrances to lowest two levels of the main tower, and a stair leads up from the upper doorway to a spiral stair in the east corner. See page 56.

DUNWORLY   W480358

A tower measuring 5.8m by 5m and a 4m long section of curtain wall 1m thick closed the neck of a coastal promontory. The east end of the tower basement has doorways set opposite each other in the north and south walls, and there is also one double-splayed loop facing south. Nothing now remains above a vault of slabs carried on two pointed arches across the basement. The castle belonged either to the O'Cowhigs or the Barry Roe clan.

GLANDORE   W222354

The south end of a two storey embattled mansion overlooking the harbour incorporates a 16th century O'Donovan tower measuring 12m by 9.8m. The east and west walls each have a gable-shaped recess with a gunloop in the apex. The eastern one defends the entrance doorway. The second storey has a blocked ogival-headed loop with recessed spandrels. A turret projects from the NW corner. Glandore was sold to the Tonsons in the 18th century, and later passed to the FitzWilliam Barrys and then the MacCarthys.

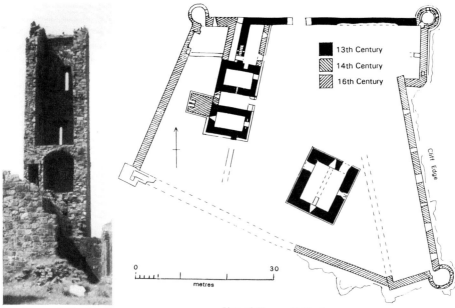

13th Century
14th Century
16th Century

Glanworth Castle   *Plan of Glanworth Castle*

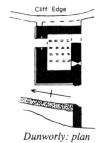

Dunworly: plan

Dunworly Castle

GLANWORTH R758041 A

Excavations have shown that the Condons' original 13th century castle on a cliff above the River Funshion had a trapezoidal court with a rectangular gatehouse measuring 16m by 9m on the west side with guardrooms on either side of a central passage. In the later medieval period the gatehouse was converted into a tower house with an added battered base and its passageway outer arch blocked by the addition of a projecting latrine turret, now the highest part of the building, since the only the lower parts survive of the rest. A range was built over the stump of the west curtain wall north of the gatehouse and a new outer curtain wall 1.7m thick built further west to enlarge the court. A new gateway was inserted in the 1.5m thick north curtain wall, which is still mostly original 13th century work. The east and south walls of the court were later rebuilt, the east side having several openings serving a former 40m long building there, probably a ground level hall with chambers at one or both ends. There are thinly walled 16th century circular flankers up to 5.5m in diameter containing gunloops at the NW, NE and SE corners at the court, whilst the SW corner has the base of a square turret. Lying isolated within the court not far from the south side is a two storey 13th century keep measuring 12.6m by 10.8m over walls 2.1m thick above a battered base. It contains a chamber with a SW corner latrine over a cellar with four loops, each level having its own doorway in the north wall. The lower room was later subdivided by a crosswall to carry vaults, now destroyed. Glanworth passed to the Roches in the 14th century and was held by them until confiscated by Cromwell in the 1650s. The site remained at least partly occupied into the 18th century.

Glanworth Castle

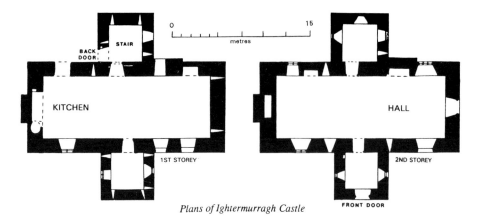

Plans of Ightermurragh Castle

IGHTERMURRAGH   W991724

This is an impressive four storey stronghouse with a main block 21.8m by 9.6m over walls 1.6m thick with a wing 5.8m wide projecting 5m from the centres of the south and north sides to make a cruciform plan. The whole building has string-courses between the storeys and retains its wall-walks and the lower part of the parapets. At that level there is a machicolation upon pyramidal corbels above the main entrance set at second storey level in the end wall of the south wing, where it could not otherwise be covered by the many gunloops in the wings. The north wing contained a timber stair with a service doorway at its foot. This doorway is covered by two gunloops and had a drawbar, as did the inner doorway from the wing into the main block. A projecting breast at the west end contains a large fireplace with a side-oven for the ground level kitchen in the main block. Six out of the original seven chimney stacks still remain. The upper levels each contained a large room on either side of a central lobby with timber partition walls. These levels had windows of one, two and three lights, the larger ones having transoms. Most of the long lintels which covered the embrasures internally have been removed. A stone plaque over the main entrance has been removed but the fireplace on the north side of the main hall in the eastern part of second storey has a joggled lintel with a Latin inscription declaring that "Edmund Supple and Margaret (Fitz)Gerald, whom love binds as one, built this house in 1642". The name Ightermurragh comes from the Gaelic for "the lower is my choice", which Margaret is supposed to have said to her father Edmund when he was allocating his lands amongst his three daughters. Soon after completion the house was captured and burnt but it was restored and in the mid 18th century was occupied by a Mr Smith.

INCHICRENAGH or CASTLE RICHARD   X011737   D

In the farmyard of Castle Richard stands a 20m high tower measuring 13.8m by 10.2m with barrel-vaults over the second and fourth of five storeys. The doorway at the west end of the north wall bears the date 1592 and initials T.G. for Thomas FitzGerald, but the tower lacks fireplaces or gunloops and was probably built in the 1430s or 40s by Richard FitzGerald, first seneschal of Imokilly. The pointed-headed doorway between the entrance lobby and the cellar has a portcullis groove. A straight stair covered by a murder-hole leads up to where a spiral stair begins in the NE corner. The third storey has loops on all four sides, the northern one having access to a latrine in the NW corner. The 1.3m thick side walls of the fifth storey are in a precarious condition. All four sides had centrally-placed windows with paired ogival-headed lights, and there is another mural chamber in the 2.9m thick north end wall. This wall continues up above the main wall-walk, now parapet-less.

Inchicrenagh Castle

Ightermurragh Castle

INCHIQUIN   W038748

Beside a house by the Womanagh river is a badly cracked circular tower keep two storeys high with remains of a plaster finish both internally and externally. The lower room with three loops measures 9.2m in diameter and has walling up to 4.3m thick where the facing of the battered plinth remains intact. On the south side was an entrance doorway with its sill somewhat above ground level. From it rose a mural stair leading to a spiral stair to the summit. The upper room is 10.6m in diameter within walling 2.5m thick. There is a fireplace on the west flanked on one side by a window and on the other by a latrine passage. Another window embrasure facing NE has seats. The keep is mentioned as a possession of Richard de Clare at his death in 1321, and in 1350 was said to be worth nothing because it required "great repair". Renovation eventually carried out included the insertion of a dome-vault, now fallen, over the lower storey. The widow of the last Earl of Desmond lived here until her death in 1604, although Sir Richard Boyle was then the owner, having bought it in 1602 from Sir Walter Raleigh. The building is said to have been damaged by Cromwellian cannon in 1649. See plans and photograph on page 64.

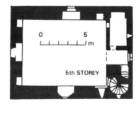

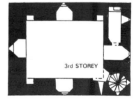

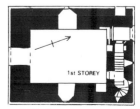

Plans of Inchicrenagh Castle

Fireplace at Kanturk

Inchiquin Castle

JAMES' FORT   W646496   A

In 1602-4 the government built a pentagonal bastioned earthwork fort about 100m across beside Kinsale harbour on a site previously occupied by a small tower. In 1611 the fort was strengthened with a stone gatehouse on the south side and a stone inner fort 40m by 30m with a demi-bastion as each corner and a loopholed wall was built in the middle. Inside the inner fort are two low rectangular towers at diagonally opposite corners of a court with three ranges. A covered way leads out to the NE towards a blockhouse on the shore. The fort was captured fairly easily by Williamite forces in 1690.

KANTURK   R383018   A

This stronghouse was begun by Dermot MacDonagh MacCarthy in 1609, having made his peace with the government after capture following the defeat at Kinsale in 1601. The shell stands to its full height of three storeys of fine rooms over a low basement but the building is thought to have never been roofed (no gables or chimney stacks remain). Either Dermot was unable to borrow any more money, or the Privy Council had doubts about the building's purpose and had work on it terminated before the intended machicolated parapet all round the building could be added upon the still surviving pyramidal corbels. Dermot took part in the wars of the 1640s but by then had mortgaged his lands to Sir Philip Percival. Bold mouldings divide the storeys externally, and the upper rooms have three-light mullion-and-transom windows with hoodmoulds, whilst there is an ornate doorway in the middle of the NW side, where the base batter is discontinued and there was intended to be a bawn. There are gunloops at ground level in the four corner towers, which are 8.4m square, and have four upper levels with two-light windows and corner fireplaces. The main block measures 27 by 11m over walls 1.3m thick and has upper level fireplaces near the ends of the east and west walls. The basement has doorways on both sides, one of them below the ornate doorway, and on the SE side there is a kitchen fireplace.

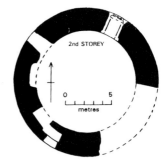

Plans of Inchiquin Castle

2nd STOREY

1st STOREY

0   5
m

Doorway at Kanturk

Plans of Kanturk Castle

Kanturk Castle

Kilbolane Castle   *Kilbolane Castle*

KILBOLANE   R423210   A

A court about 45m square enclosed by walls 1.6m thick was built here in the 13th century, probably by Maurice de Rochford. It passed to Thomas MacShane FitzGibbon in the late 14th century. After the FitzGibbons were forfeited in 1587 the castle was granted to Hugh Cuffe, but the FitzGibbon heiress, Helena, and her husband William Power later recovered it. The castle was damaged in the wars of the 1640s and then went to John Nichols, who lived in a house beside the lost eastern tower. The castle passed to his grandson John Bowen, who in the 1690s demolished much of it to provide material for a new house to the NW. The remaining parts survived because the south tower had been sold to the Weekes family and they also claimed the west tower (then known as Brandon's Castle), resulting in a dispute that proved costly for the Bowens.

The remains comprise the west corner tower 7.2m in diameter above a battered base, the south corner tower 6m in diameter above its base, the curtain wall between them with a ditch in front and a long length of the NW curtain. Neither tower projected boldly outside the curtains, so they lay partly within the court, towards which they have straight fronts. The west tower has two dome-vaulted rooms connected by a mural stair on the south side, the upper room having one ogival-headed loop, and its vault being perhaps a later insertion. The south tower was remodelled in the later medieval period and remained occupied until the 1690s. Both the vaults here may be insertions, the lower one being an unusual shape. Beside a NW-facing loop a long passage in a thicker and higher section of the curtain led out onto the main curtain wall-walk. Another long passage higher up led to a latrine. There is a spiral stair where the SE curtain once adjoined the tower.

KILBRITTAIN   W531471

Kilbrittain was the principal seat of MacCarthy Riabhach from the early 16th century until it was surrendered in 1642 after being bombarded with cannon, but the de Courcys are thought to have had a castle here by 1295 when they were defeated nearby by the MacCarthys. The two families fiercely disputed possession of it for many years and in 1414 the castle was stormed by James FitzGerald, Earl of Desmond, who removed Diarmuid an Duna MacCarthy in favour of Diarmuid's elder brother Donogh. However the Donogh soon lost the castle to John de Courcy Baron Kinsale. De Courcy in turn lost the castle in 1449, but regained it in 1462. An 18th and 19th century mansion created out of the ruins by the Stalwell family was burnt in 1920 but the east end of the south range, in which lies the vaulted lowest storey of the tower house, was restored as a residence in 1969. It has a north doorway, a few steps of a former spiral stair in the NE corner, and original loops facing north and east. From the lost upper parts of the tower has probably come a keystone from a fireplace now in the grounds of Upton House, near Ishannon. It is dated 1596 with a Latin inscription recording the tower as having been built by Donal MacCarthy and Margaret FitzGerald. Also of that period is the circular tower 6m in diameter containing several gunloops at the SE corner of the yard to the east.

KILCOE   W019328

At the north end of an island on the north shore of Roaringwater Bay is a tower of the Clan Dermot branch of MacCarthy Riabhach. Sir Richard Perry led some of the Kinsale garrison in an attempt to capture the castle in 1600. Conor O'Driscoll fled to the castle with a ward of the Earl of Thomond, who began a siege in April 1602. Captain Harvey continued the siege but failed to take it and the garrison only finally surrendered in February 1603 to Captain Flower. The tower measures 12m by 10m and has storeys but the wing 6.2m square clasping its NE corner contains six levels of small rooms. From the uppermost of two south-facing doorways into the lowest levels a stair leads up around the SE corner to the topmost room. The second storey has mural passages but no surviving windows, and the vaulted third storey loft also lacks any windows. The top room has a large central window on each side, the western one having embrasure seats, while the southern one is flanked by carved heads. A passage leads to the second level of the wing, below which is a vaulted prison reached only by a trapdoor. Another passage leads to the wing third storey room. The fourth storey of the wing is reached directly from the main block topmost room. A stair leads round from the south facing window up to the wing fifth storey room and then a stair leads from there to the room above.

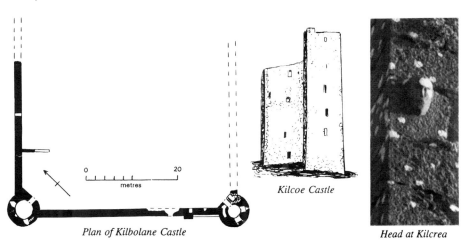

Plan of Kilbolane Castle

Kilcoe Castle

Head at Kilcrea

Kilcrea Castle

Kilcolman Castle

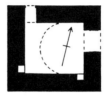

Kilgobbin: plan

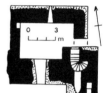

Kilcolman: plan

KILCOLMAN   R580113

This tower was built by the Earl of Desmond after he acquired the estate from the Barrys in 1430. It measures about 8.2m square but the west wall is defaced and the north wall has been patched up in the 19th century. The SE corner is clasped by a turret, giving space for third and fourth storey latrines in addition to a spiral stair. Only the turret and the south wall still stand above the vault over the second storey, which was a loft reached only by a hatch from below. The tower lay in the Sw corner of a bawn 50m by 30m now only indicated by footings and two low fragments of eastern corner turrets. The castle was granted to Edmund Spenser in 1590. Here he wrote most of his long allegorical poem "The Faerie Queen", but in 1598 he was ejected and the castle burnt.

KILCREA   W506683   D

On top of a low ditched mound lies a tower measuring 14.8m by 11.2m and a later bawn of similar size east of it. The bawn has a wall 6m high and 1.4m thick now broken down where it met the main tower. A latrine chute on the north, one window on the east and two cupboards suggest the former presence of lean-to buildings against the wall, and there is a two storey tower 5.4m wide projecting 3.8m from the south end of the east side. The lower room once had a vault. A doorway from the wall-walk led into the upper room, which has several windows, one facing west having flanking gunloops, now blocked.

There are cruciform loops in the second storey of the main tower, two facing east and south where the stair from the entrance meets the start of the spiral stair in the SE corner, and two more facing east and north in a mural room off the east window of the vaulted main chamber. This room also has a murder-hole over the entrance below. At third storey level the main room has an ogival-headed south loop and there are L-shaped rooms in three corners, that to the NE having a latrine. The fourth storey has a vault and windows at each end of two lights. The windows in the centre of each side of the fifth storey were pairs of ogival-headed lights under hoodmoulds. A fireplace was later inserted into the west side of the north window embrasure. From the east embrasure there is access to a latrine in the NE corner and a stair to the wall-walk, which now lacks its parapet. Cormac Laidir MacCarthy is said to have built this tower and the nearby friary in the 1460s.

KILGOBBIN   W589499

Abandoned farm buildings adjoin a five storey MacCarthy Riabhach tower beside the west bank of the Bandon. The tower measures 10.2m by 9m over walls 1.8m thick and is now entered through a broken loop in the east wall, the entrance doorway in the north wall being blocked. The second storey barrel-vaulted loft with a trapdoor near the SW corner. The fourth storey is also vaulted and has several square-headed loops. The fifth storey has remains of an east window of three ogival-headed lights, single ogival-headed lights in the other walls, and a spiral stair up to the wall-walk at the NE corner. The castle passed to the Sarsfields in the early 17th century and was later held by the Palmer family.

Top storey of Kilcrea Castle

Kilgobbin Castle

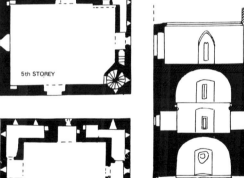

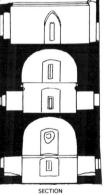

SECTION

Kilnatoora Castle

5th STOREY

3rd STOREY

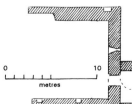

1st STOREY

0   10
metres

Kilcrea: plans & section

KILMACLENINE   R504061

On a ridge is a roughly rectangular court 40m long east-west by 30m wide with low fragments of a wall 1.3m thick built on top of low cliffs. Part of the east side and the SW corner are missing. There is a projecting spur at the east end of the north wall and a turret (probably a latrine) further west. A ramp at the west end of the south side marks the former entrance. The court may be 13th century in date. It has no internal structures and may have simply provided a refuge for the tenants of the bishops of Cloyne. See page 8.

On the south side of a farmyard barely 100m to the NE is a stronghouse assumed to have been built by the Barrys in the 1630s, similar in layout and size to the cruciform house at Ightermurragh but lower, having just two upper storeys divided externally by a stringcourse set over a low basement. The main block has several fireplace and mullion-and-transom windows, one on the south side being of three lights. The main block measures 21.6m long by 10.6m wide and the wings are 6m wide with a projection of 5m. The east end has gone, and most of the north wing collapsed c1870, which a chimney stack on the south wing fell in 1902. There is a recess for an armorial plaque over the doorway in the end wall of this wing in which are gunloops flanking the main block.

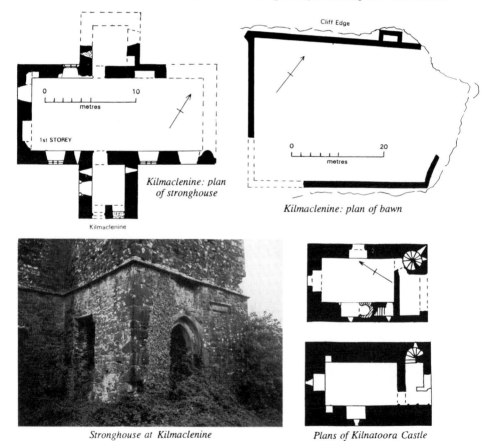

Kilmaclenine: plan
of stronghouse

Kilmaclenine

Kilmaclenine: plan of bawn

Stronghouse at Kilmaclenine

Plans of Kilnatoora Castle

Bawn at Kilmaclenine

KILMEEDY   W264877

This round-cornered tower measuring 13.3m by 10.2m was built by the MacCarthys of Drishane probably c1550-1600 to guard a pass between the Musherabeg and Claragh mountains. The east wall contains the entrance and a tier of mural chambers reached from a spiral stair in the SE corner. There are vaults over the second and fourth of five storeys. The third storey has a fireplace on the north and a passage to a room in a former SW bartizan. At this level the east mural chamber has access to a room in a more complete bartizan on the NE corner with gunloops and machicolations. The fourth storey has a mural room in the NW corner.

KILNATOORA   X058800   D

The south wall of this tower of a branch of the Imokilly FitzGeralds has collapsed, having been breached by cannon in an attack by Lord Castlehaven in 1645, but the staircase in the SE corner is still intact. Quarrying seems to have removed the remains of a bawn with a round SE flanker depicted by Grose. The tower measures 14.5m by 8.6m and has its north end backing onto a 10m high cliff above the valley of the River Tourig. The fallen wall contained the entrance and a tier of mural chambers above, the lowest of which had a murder hole covering the entrance lobby. It is likely there was a second entrance above directly into the vaulted second storey. The west window of the third storey main room was later adapted as a fireplace with an adjoining oven, the flue partly blocking the passage to a fourth storey latrine in the NW corner. The fifth storey above a second vault also has a latrine in the NW corner. The main room has east and west windows with paired ogival-headed lights, plus a single light facing north. Two chimney stacks block the western wall-walk. The SE corner still retains its parapet. See page 69.

KINSALE   W635505   C

The walls here are first mentioned as being ruinous in 1333 and were probably begun in the mid 13th century. A grant for repairing them was made in 1348. The walls played a part in the battle of Kinsale in 1601 and were much damaged during a siege by Williamite forces in 1690. A long low section of the north wall still remains. There were once four gates in the main part and two more in a narrow southern suburb called Base Town which was walled in the late 16th century. In Cork Street is a three storey tower known as Desmond Castle or the French Prison, having served as a prison from the 1630s until c1800, mostly for foreign captives. The upper storeys have two-light windows, those of the second level having ogival heads and featuring two set at angles with the mullions forming angles of the building. The fine basement doorway may be a later insertion.

Liscarroll: gatehouse

Leitrim Castle

LEITRIM   R862010   D

A 13th or 14th century wall 1.6m thick and up to 4m high surrounds a bawn 33m square, the SE corner being missing and the NE corner very ruined. Projecting slightly from the SW corner was a rectangular block about 14m long by 7.5m wide with a pair of pointed-headed recesses at the south end. Various ruined openings suggest that there were ranges of buildings all along the north and east sides, with arcading in the NE corner and a fireplace in the middle of the east side. This Condon seat passed after their attainder in 1597 to the Sherlocks. They in turn were attainted, and in 1657 Leitrim was granted to the Campions, who held it until 1875.

LICKLASH   W828999   D

A five storey 16th century tower 6.2m square above a battered base is partly built over the north wall of a hall probably of 13th century date of which the east wall with two tall slit windows still stands. Further south are fragments of a bawn wall (with a possible gunloop) set on a cliff edge above the north side of the Blackwater river. The tower would have flanked the vanished 5m high and 0.9m thick west wall of the bawn. It has vaults over the second and fourth levels. A wooden stair now leads up through the lower vault. A spiral stair in the NE corner then leads to the upper levels. A sketch of 1844 shows the hall much more complete with a turret at its south end. The castle belonged to the Roches but passed to the Hendleys in the 17th century.

Liscarroll Castle   *Licklash Castle*

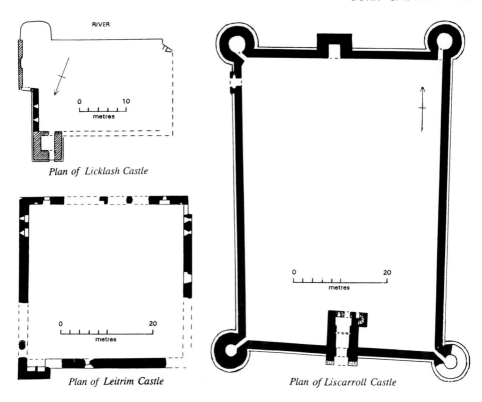

RIVER

Plan of Licklash Castle

Plan of Leitrim Castle

Plan of Liscarroll Castle

LISCARROLL   R452124   B

This late 13th century castle of the Barrys was acquired by Sir Philip Percival in 1620s after being mortgaged to him by John Barry. It consists of a court 62m by 50m enclosed by a 7m high curtain wall 2m thick with a round tower 8m in diameter at each corner, a tower 9m wide projecting 3m from the north wall, and a rectangular gatehouse measuring 12m by 7m on the south side. The loss of the curtain on either side of the gatehouse and the near total destruction of the SE tower (said to have contained a well) is the result of a bombardment by the Cromwellian Sir Hardress Waller in 1650 and subsequent slighting. The castle had previously endured a thirteen day siege in 1642 by a Confederate army led by Gerald Barry, only to be immediately retaken by Lord Inchiquin. The corner towers each have three storeys with doorways from the court to the lowest two levels. From the upper doorways stairs lead to the top storeys and the curtain wall-walks. The ruinous turret just south of the NW tower contained an upper level latrine. There may have been another just north of the SW tower where the curtain now has a large patch.

The gatehouse projects mostly within the curtain and had a domestic block extending from its west side to the curtain west wall. Over a long passage it contained a fine upper chamber reached by a spiral stair in a turret on the NE corner. Later medieval windows with pairs of ogival-headed lights and seats in the embrasures face south, east and north. There are doorways to the curtain wall-walks, and access to a latrine contrived at a different level on the west, and there was a fireplace in the west wall. The passageway portcullis was operated from the south window embrasure. This end of the building is vaulted to carry an extra half storey added in the 15th or 16th century. From the north window embrasure stairs led to a chamber at the top of the stair turret.

Liscarroll Castle

LISGRIFFIN   R487085   D

More survived in 1865 but all that now remains of a 10m wide stronghouse built by the Barrys in the early 17th century is the west wall, standing complete with remains of central mullioned windows on each of three storeys and a gable with a chimney within a very ruinous machicolated parapet set upon a row of eight pyramidal corbels. A stub of the north wall contains a ground level gunloop close to the corner. The house was granted to William Grove in the 1650s, but was soon transferred to Major Ion.

Lisgriffin Castle   *Lohort Castle*

LOHORT R465014

This round-cornered MacDonagh MacCarthy tower measuring 13.6m by 10.2m passed "in default" to Sir Philip Percival in 1641. He probably constructed the corner-bastioned fort shown surrounding the tower in a drawing of c1750 which depicts an outer moat (now vanished) around the fort and the circular inner moat 4m wide still surrounding tower. After being captured by the Irish the castle was bombarded and retaken in 1650 by a Cromwellian force but shows no obvious scars of this incident. The tower was renovated in the 1740s by the Earl of Egmont as a residence for his agent and remained in use until burnt in 1922. The stepped east gable and the chimney stacks date 1876, and some renovation has been carried out more recently. A stair leads from the entrance in the east end wall to a spiral stair in the SE corner. There are five storeys, with vaults over the first and third, the lower vault having a central pier, probably not an original arrangement. Two of the upper mural chambers in the east wall have mullioned windows with hoodmoulds, perhaps 17th century insertions. The windows of paired ogival-headed lights in the other walls appear to be 18th or 19th century rather than medieval. A machicolated parapet is carried round the entire summit except for a gap on the east side. This parapet is carried up at a higher level where it meets the head of the stair at the SE corner. See pages 5 and 74.

2nd STOREY

Lisgriffin: plan

1st STOREY

Lohort: plan

MACRONEY R854024

This Condon tower above the Araglin river was granted to the Manserghs in the late 17th century. Their crest appears in the keystone of the entrance on the south side, now covered by a new porch. Recent renovation by the Hamiltons has also resulted in new upper windows, the addition of a two storey annex on the east, and a pair of single storey extensions on the north. The tower now has three storeys crowned by new crenellated parapets around a hipped roof. The SW corner has a square bartizan on three pyramidal corbels and corbels remain for a similar bartizan at the NE corner.

MACROOM W338729

A technical school south of the bridge over the River Sullane lies on the site of a mansion of several periods incorporating a tower house and other old parts of an important seat of the MacCarthys of Muskerry. Lord Broghill defeated a royalist force here in 1649, the Bishop of Rosscarbery being captured (see Carrigadrohid). Macroom was granted to the Penn family (see Shanagarry) but was later returned to Lord Muskerry. The mansion was burnt in 1922 and demolished c1967.

Macroney Castle

Mashanaglass Castle

Mallow Castle

MALLOW   W570977   A

A low fragment on the end of the promontory above the Blackwater may be a relic of a 13th century Roche castle. A description of 1584 suggests there was once a five storey tower house and a separate hall set over a vaulted basement, as well as a bawn and outer enclosures. The short section of thick walling adjoining the stronghouse NE corner could also be a relic of the older building.

The stronghouse on the neck of the promontory was built either by Sir Thomas Norris, or by his daughter and her Jephson husband after the burning of the town in 1598. It held out against Lord Mountgarret in 1642 but was captured by Lord Castlehaven in 1645. After the castle was burnt by Jacobites in 1689 the Jephsons made themselves a more modest house out of the stable block 70m further north. The stronghouse is a three storey structure 27.2m long by 10.6m wide with semi-polygonal wings projecting from the middle of each side and hexagonal turrets bodly projecting from the NW and SW corners. A lower annex to the south contained a kitchen with a fireplace in the north wall. There is another large ground level kitchen in the east wall of the northern part of the house. The central west wing contains the entrance doorway on its north side and there is a back doorway towards the bawn on the promontory on the east side, both doorways having drawbar slots. The NW turret contained a spiral stair and there was probably a scale-and-platt stair in the east wing, with latrines in the pointed end beyond. The lowest windows are of two lights, those above lighting the main living rooms were of three with transoms, and those lighting the bedrooms were of two lights with transoms. On the west and north sides some of the windows have stirrup-shaped gunloops below them. In the town, not far to the NW, lay a second fortified building called Short Castle or Castle Gar, destroyed after the fighting here in 1642.

MANNING   R771031

Of a Condon castle granted in 1588 to Arthur Hyde there remain only 3m high fragments with one jamb of a doorway, and piles of debris from a tower lying at the SW corner of a bawn about 55m by 45m now only marked by buried footings.

MARYBROOK   R433048

The existing house with early 19th century features, but possibly of 17th century origin, incorporates thick walls of a 16th century tower with the outline of a removed doorway on the north side and corbels for a third storey level bartizan.

MASHANAGLASS   W370707   C

This late 16th century MacCarthy castle was held for them by the MacSweeneys, who later became its legal owners. Of a tower measuring 13.5m by 9.4m four storeys survive but little remains of the east wall containing the entrance and mural chambers, and nothing at all of the staircase in the SE corner, which was blown up c1864. The vaulted second storey has access to vaulted rooms with gunloops within triangular spurs projecting from the NE and SW corners. The spurs have solid bases and were themselves flanked by recessed angled gunloops in the main block. The third and fourth storeys have fireplaces in the north wall, and the third storey has a south window of two ogival-headed lights under a hoodmould. See page 79.

Mallow Castle

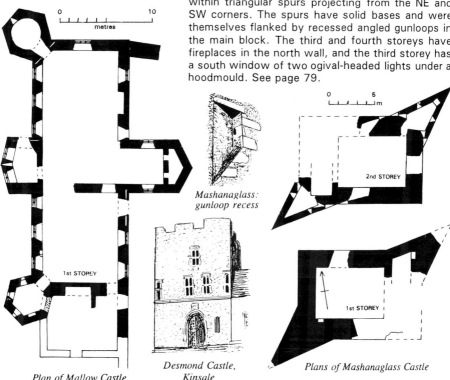

Plan of Mallow Castle

Mashanaglass: gunloop recess

Desmond Castle, Kinsale

Plans of Mashanaglass Castle

MOGEELEY   W957941   C

A bawn about 45m square on a rock above the flood plain of the Bride river contains 19th and 20th century farm buildings. There seems to have been a small east projection at the NE corner, and nearby is latrine turret added to the 5m high north wall. The 4m high west wall lies beyond what remains of the west end wall of a 13th century two storey keep measuring about 17m by 10m on the south side. The north wall has gone but the south wall retains one upper window embrasure partly visible above a lean-to shed. The latrine turret at the SW corner is a later addition. The castle is first mentioned in 1464 when the Earl of Desmond acquired it from the Knight of Kerry. It was besieged and captured during the rebellion of 1579 and later given to Sir Walter Raleigh. An English garrison withstood a four month siege here in 1598-9. The castle formed the official residence of William St Leger, Lord President of Munster from 1610 to 1628. It was bombarded and captured in 1645 by the Earl of Castlehaven. It later went to the Boyles, earls of Cork, and passed to the Duke of Devonshire in 1707, although it was then held by the Paynes as tenants.

MONANIMY   R651000   C

Recently restored as a residence, this Nagle castle later held by the Riggs's and the Haliburtons looks like a 17th century remodelling of a late medieval structure, but alterations were also made c1810 by William Barry. The original east-facing doorway has now been made into a window and the existing doorway faces north. Wooden steps in the SW corner lead to the second storey, which has an inserted doorway on the east side reached by an external flight of steps. Off the wooden internal stair is a passage to a narrow spiral stair connecting four rooms in a turret 4.2m by 3.7m boldly projecting at the SW corner. The lowest of the turret rooms is only just above ground level and has three gunloops. At the NE corner there is access to a tiny room inside a circular turret just 2.5m in diameter, and to steps leading to a latrine at a higher level in the north wall. The third storey main room has a three-light window with a hoodmould facing east and a two-light window facing south. The fourth storey features are all 19th or 20th century.

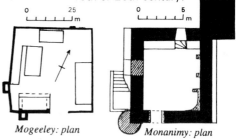

Mogeeley: plan   Monanimy: plan

Monanimy Castle

Mogeeley Castle

Monkstown Castle

MONKSTOWN   W766662   C

Overlooking the south entrance of the West Passage of Cork Harbour is a derelict stronghouse built in the 1630s by the Archdeacon family. It has a three storey main block 14m by 8.8m with four boldly projecting corner towers 7.5m square, all the walls being 1.2m thick and having stringcourses marking divisions between storeys. The towers have four storeys and an attic within a roof with four gables, the innermost two of which have chimneys, whilst the outermost corner of each tower has a square open bartizan carried on five pyramidal corbels. The elliptical-arched main entrance faces north. Two similar service doorways into the west towers are covered by an arch upon which the west end of the main block is brought forward at the upper levels. There are tiers of two-light windows with step-ended hoodmoulds, many now lacking their mullions and the lower ones blocked up. One second storey window in the main block is of three lights with a transom. There are many gunloops at ground level, where there is a large kitchen fireplace in the main block west wall. Above is an more elaborate fireplace dated 1636 and 1814 with initials of Bernard Shaw, who renovated the building. It was later used as an army barracks and then passed to Lord De Vesci, who added various outbuildings in 1873. It later served as a golf clubhouse but was superseded by a new clubhouse in 1971 and then abandoned.

MONTEEN   W431470

Beside a ruined 18th century house is a tower measuring just 6m by 5.6m, seat of Florence Riabhach MacCarthy when burnt by Captain Flower in 1600. His heirs later held it as tenants of the Coppingers. The segmental vault of the cellar has a gap of 0.6m between it and the north wall. A similar gap between the third storey vault and the east wall is covered by overlapping slabs. Originally there was another storey above. The upper two levels have doorways in the south wall.

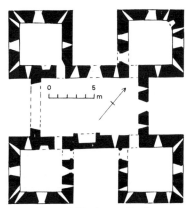

Plans of Monkstown Castle

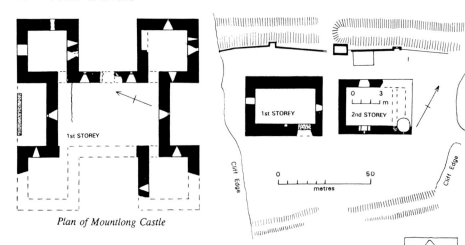

Plan of Mountlong Castle

1st STOREY

1st STOREY

2nd STOREY

Cliff Edge

Cliff Edge

0   50
metres

Old Head: plans and section

MOSSGROVE   W431604

A much rebuilt wall 3m high links two circular towers 4m in diameter which marked the western side of a bawn. The southern tower contains a gunloop in the form of a slit with D-shaped ends. Only buried footings remain of a house with wings extending 18m to the south and west of a tower in the bawn NE corner. The east wall was 1.2m thick. This was the 17th century seat of the Baldwin family, who later moved to Mount Pleasant House.

MOUNTLONG   W676511

The stronghouse built by John Long in 1631 was only occupied for about a dozen years before being burnt during the conflicts of the 1640s. Scars of the fire remain on the wooden lintels of the embrasures of the tiers of two-light windows with hoodmoulds. One second storey window is of three lights. The house was almost a twin of the stronghouse at Monkstown, having towers 6.5m square at all four corners of a main block 13.2m long by 9.2m wide over walls 1.2m thick. There are gunloops at ground level and under the sills of some of the upper windows. The entrance on the east is now just a gap. The western towers are very ruined but the east towers still stand three full storeys with string-courses between them, with attic rooms within the four-gabled roofs. The inner gables have chimney stacks but there are no bartizans like those at Monkstown.

Old Head of Kinsale

Mountlong Castle

OLDCOURT   W083319

On the east shore of the estuary of the River Ilen lies an O'Driscoll tower captured by the English after the battle of Kinsale. It measures 9m by 7.3m and lies in the SE corner of a very ruined and altered bawn. The west end wall contains doorways into the lowest two levels, the uppermost of which is vaulted and has a fireplace. The upper doorway leads to a chamber from which the portcullis of the lower doorway was operated. A straight stair in the north wall leads to a spiral stair in the NW corner providing access to two more storeys under a now destroyed upper vault, and a lost fifth storey on top. The third storey has a chamber in the west wall, window embrasures with seats, and a small fireplace.

OLD HEAD OF KINSALE or DUNMACPATRICK   W624409   A

The 120m wide neck of the Old Head of Kinsale has ditch up to 15m wide and 2.5m deep with a retaining wall on the southern inner side. Much of the wall is now level with the internal ground level but there is a 3.5m high section just west of the road leading through the site out to the modern lighthouse. A lost gateway where the road passes through was protected by a tower house to the east, beyond which to the east there is the base of a building which probably contained a hall 11m long by 5.3m wide against the 1.2m thick curtain wall. Further east is the lower part of a tower 5.3m wide. There is also a small intermediate turret flanking the western section of the wall. About 70m further south the headland is isolated by another rock-cut ditch up to 4m deep with evidence of a 1m high rampart on its north side. Although the site was probably fortified from an early date, the existing defences appear to have been built in the 15th century by the de Courcy family, the lofty main tower probably additionally functioning as a lighthouse. The site was seized by the English in 1600. Further inland is one of the series of signal towers of the 1790s.

   The tower house measures 6.2m by 8.3m and rises 13.2m to a narrow wall-walk now lacking a parapet. A stair in the SE corner is reached from the uppermost of two doorways in the south wall. The second storey has a vault which stops short of the east wall, the gap probably being originally covered with slabs. Above the vault was a private room with windows with embrasure seats facing south and north and an arch at the east end to carry a platform rising another 2.8m above the wall-walk. Originally there was a similar arch and platform at the west end, with the wall-walk carried through it as a passage.

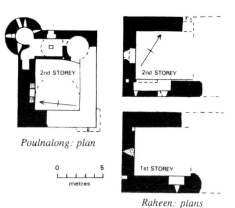

Poulnalong: plan

0   5
metres

Raheen: plans

POULNALONG   W571551   B

Raheen Castle

Between a road and the east bank of the Banson River is a tower measuring 10.4m by 8.6m over walls 1.8m thick which was built under royal licence in the 1540s by Philip Roche. A hundred rebel Irish were killed when the castle was captured in 1642 by the garrison of Bandon. Also known as Shippool, it was inhabited by the Merrick family until they moved elsewhere in 1787 and seems to have stood complete in 1907. A gable then survived on the now fallen upper part of the west wall, the debris of which fills the lower interior. There is a pointed arched doorway facing the river but there could be another entrance doorway buried under the roadway on the east side where the upper wall contains mural chambers and the well of a wide spiral stair in the SE corner which connected the third, fourth and fifth levels. This side was flanked by a 4m diameter circular turret set on the NE corner to contain two levels of gunloops, the upper ones being steeply angled downwards. The second storey main room has a fireplace, ogival-headed loops facing north and south and a gap on the west where an oriel window overlooked the river. Just one corbel remains of a square bartizan on the SW corner at third storey level.

RAHEEN   W193320

The east wall of this tower is entirely destroyed and the lowest level is mostly buried with debris but the other walls stand four storeys high with a gable of a fifth storey attic on the west wall and a square bartizan on three corbels at the SW corner. The surviving walls each have a gable-shaped recess covered by a gunloop opening out from the sill of a third storey window. The west window at that level also has flanking gunloops. This storey has remains of a vault and chambers in the north and south walls, the latter having a latrine. The SE corner shows traces of the entrance doorway facing east at second storey level, where there is another mural chamber on the south. The west wall shows signs of a Cromwellian bombardment in 1649, and the interior has evidence of burning. The tower was probably built by Donal O'Donovan after he succeeded his father in 1584. His son was forfeited in the 1640s, but recovered Raheen, only for his son, another Donal, to be forfeited by the Williamites in the 1690s.

RATHBARRY or CASTLE FREKE   W322352 E

Nothing remains of the tower said to have been built here in the 15th century by Randal Oge Barry. Captain Arthur Freke purchased the property in 1641. In the following year his house and bawn here withstood a siege by the Irish Confederate forces from February until October, when a relief force arrived led by Sir Charles Vavasour and Captain Jephson. Vavasour then burned the house, but it was restored in 1643 and garrisoned by the Parliamentarian Colonel Myn. The house was again damaged by Jacobites in 1690 but remained occupied by the Frekes until the new mansion of Castle Freke was built nearby. The farm buildings in a park overlooking Lough Rahavarrig and Long Strand are mostly mid 19th century work, but on the south and west sides there is a revetment wall built against a rock face flanked on the south by a semi-hexagonal bastion with blocked gunports, now filled in up to courtyard level. There is also a round-arched gateway at the SE corner.

REENAVANNY   V974508

On a rock at the NE end of Whiddy Island is a ruinous tower measuring 10.7m by 8.6m which belonged to O'Sullivan Bere. The SW wall stands three storeys high and the NW wall with a window embrasure and one jamb of the entrance doorway stands one storey high, but the rest mostly collapsed in 1920. The castle was occupied by Carew in 1602 and was captured and wrecked by Ireton for Cromwell in 1650.

Poulnalong Castle   *Poulnalong Castle*

REENADISERT   WOO1530   D

This T-plan house overlooking the NE corner of Bantry Bay was probably built by Sir Owen O'Sullivan (d1616) to replace the castle at Dunboy destroyed in 1602. It was captured by Ireton for Cromwell in 1650. The 7.5m wide and 20.4m long eastern arm is of two storeys over a partial basement including a north end kitchen and has bartizans containing closets opening out of the upper storey rooms on the NW and SE corners. The bartizans are square but with the outer corner cut off. Later partition walls divide the interior into three units, the southern of which has two gunloops on the lowest level and is the only part still roofed. The present entrance in the middle of the east side has an external staircase. The 8m wide western arm projects 14m and also has a bartizan on the SW corner. It now contains lean-to farm buildings around a central court but originally had three storeys and an attic. On the north side of the court is a wide original fireplace in a projecting breast.

RINCOLISKY   WO17303

Only the lowest two storeys now remain of a tower above the SE side of Roaringwater Bay said to have been built in 1495 by the O'Driscolls. The upper level is vaulted and both levels have square headed loops with lintelled embrasures and doorways facing east. A a stair rises from the pointed-arched upper doorway to where the SE corner is now broken down. The castle was mortgaged to Sir Walter Coppinger, who took possession in 1628.

RINGRONE   W634487

The west wall of a de Courcy tower still stands four storeys high with evidence of vaults over the first and third levels and a doorway at the west end of the north wall.

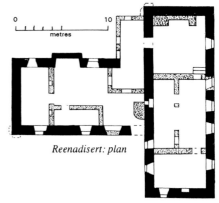

Reenadisert: plan

Ringrone Castle   *Rossmore Castle*

Bartizan at Reenadisert

Rossmore: plan

Reenadisert Castle

ROSSBRIN V978314

The easternmost of the O'Mahony castles of west Cork lies on the west side of Rossbrin Bay. After Donal O'Mahony was executed in September 1562 the citizens of Cork sent a naval force to capture the castle. It was later returned to Donal's son Cornelius but in 1571 Sir John Perrot had the castle captured by another naval force. The garrison of MacSwiney gallowglas then installed proved rebellious and the castle was returned to Conor O'Mahony in 1578. He was attainted for his part in the Earl of Desmond's rebellion of 1579, and in 1584 Rossbrin was handed over to Oliver Lambert. He surrendered the estate to the Crown in 1602 and the castle was then leased to the Morgans. The west wall collapsed in a storm in 1905. Part of the pointed vault over the third storey loft fell in 1963, and more collapsed in 1975, but the NE corner still stands four storeys high, with the head of a stair rising from the north jamb of the uppermost of two doorways in the lowest two levels in the east wall. The lower doorway is mostly blocked by rubble. Above these doorways were mural chambers.

ROSSMORE V978314 C

Of an O'Mahony tower beside Dunmanus Bay which later passed to the MacCarthy Muclaghs the 14.5m long north wall still stands three storeys high with evidence of gable-shaped gunloop recesses and a chute of a NE corner latrine. Remains of the west wall forming part of a farm building contain the blocked entrance doorway and indicate a width of about 9m. There are traces of a spiral stairwell in the NW corner.

SHANAGARRY W979666

Of a tower probably built by the Power (originally de la Poer) family in the 16th century there remain behind a Catholic church the lowest stage of the south wall and a higher fragment of the east wall, with the well of a spiral stair in the angle between them. The east wall with upper and lower fireplaces survives of a two storey wing about 7m square added to the eastern half the south side. The small gabled building further NE has gunloops on the upper level but is not shown on the 1842 map. Shanagarry passed to the Penn family in the 1660s and a house nearby was occasionally used by William Penn, the famous Quaker who founded the state of Pennsylvania in North America. See page 86.

Shanagarry Castle

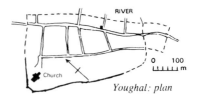

Youghal: plan

TEMPLECONNELL   R520115

This Magner castle was taken over by the Percivals in 1656. The tower lay in the SW corner of a bawn and measures 8.5m by 6.5m and is entered through the south wall. Stairs from the entrance rise to the SW corner and then double back (over a chamber with a murder hole over the entrance) to reach where a spiral stair begins in the SE corner. The first and fourth storeys have vaults and the third storey has an ogival-headed loop facing each, whilst there is a carved human head on the outside west wall at second storey level. At fourth storey level there is a chamber in the east wall with access to a latrine beyond, and a long mural chamber in the south wall. Only fragments remain of the fifth storey.

TIMOLEAGUE   W472440   C

This 15th century tower measuring 13.8m by 10.6m by the Argideen river stood four storeys high with gables and chimney stacks until the 1930s, when the two upper levels were demolished by Cork County Council after they were damaged by an explosion which also destroyed the NE corner. From the upper parts has come a window transom dated 1st August 1586 with initials of David Barry and Ellen Roche now lying by the south wall. There is a similar stone at Barryscourt. They refer to rebuilding work after David Barry burnt his own castles to prevent the English using them. The lowest level has a double-splayed loop in each of the west, north and east walls, a doorway on the south covered by a gunloop and another doorway at the south end of the east wall. The level above has a window facing south and a mural stair rising in the west wall. A second stair rises from an east facing window, south of which is a mural chamber. In 1620 Conor MacOwen Hurley managed to break into the tower, but in July 1642 it was successfully defended against an attack by Lord Forbes and a party of freebooters. Cromwell granted the castle to the Swetes. They were still here in the 18th century, using the castle as a linen mill.

TOEHEAD   W144261

Excavations in the 1950s produced pottery of the period 1550-1650 together with Civil War period circular shot and revealed the subdivided lower stage of a building containing a kitchen with an oven. The south end had collapsed into the sea. It lay at the south end of a rectangular court formed on a promontory with a ditch across the neck which was recut in the 16th century. Fragments of a curtain wall were found on the inner side of the ditch, and part of a causeway with a gap for a drawbridge. Otherwise known as Dooneendermotmore, this may have been an O'Driscoll castle also known as the Downings which was captured by Lieutenant Saunders for Carew in 1602.

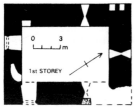

Timoleague: plan

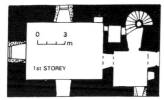

Togher: plan

Togher Castle

TOGHER   W196571   D

The MacCarthys of Glenacroim are thought to have built this four storey tower measuring 16.2m by 9.7m on a rock amongst marshland in the 1590s. It was granted to Abraham Hoare in the 1650s and retains a 19th century corrugated iron roof from when it was adapted for local industrial use. The Entrance faces east and off it rises an unusually wide stair spiralling up around a column 0.9m in diameter in the NE corner. A room beside the foot of the stair may have been a prison. The basement loops have all been broken out. The upper levels all have pairs of windows in the north and south walls and fireplaces at the east end. Over the entrance lobby is a tier of chambers, the second storey room being vaulted, and the third storey room, which has a fireplace, being locally known as the "nurse's chamber". Pyramidal corbels support bartizans on the NW and SE corners. There are chimney stacks on the end gables and a larger one above the internal partition wall.

WALLINGSTOWN   W745719   C

In an industrial estate on Little Island stands a tower whose name suggests a link with the Wallyns family, although it was held by the FitzGeralds in the 16th century and in 1678 went to the Pigots, from whom it passed to Lord Lisle and then the Burys. The tower measures 7.6m by 6m and has separate doorways into each of the lowest three levels, one at ground level on the north and the other two on the south. The top doorway has corbels for a fore-stair and gives access to a straight stair in the east wall up to the fourth storey room lying over a vault. At this level the north wall has gone and the others were later modified to take a new roof, now gone.

WALLSTOWN   R663072

The west wall 11.5m long stands to full height and has a chimney stack for a blocked fireplace at the 4th storey level. Projecting from the north end of it is a wing now containing just one vaulted room over a solid base in which is a chute for a latrine. A length of the south wall also stands to the height of a wall-walk with two gunloops in its parapet. Held by the Walls as tenants of the Roches, the tower was captured and burnt in 1642, and later given to Andrew Ruddock. It then passed to the Creaghs and Stawells.

WHITE CASTLE or ARDCLOYNE   W604516

The thin and leaning west end wall of the 9m wide stronghouse built in the early 17th century by the Roches of Kinsale has a gunloop in lowest storey, a fireplace on the third storey and a square SW corner bartizan supported upon pyramidal corbels.

YOUGHAL   X102783   C

On the NE side of Main Street, near the shore, stands a much altered 15m high tower house measuring about 12m by 7m built by the Walshes. They were forfeited in 1584, and the tower is now named after a later owner, Sir Robert Tynte, married to the Earl of Cork's daughter Elizabeth. It is of four storeys with vaults over the first and third. As a result of its use as a grain store there is a large vertical opening with doors in the front elevation.

The town was walled from 1275 onwards when there was a murage grant. There were north and south gates, neither of which remain (there is a gateway of 1776 on the site of the latter), but a plain rebuilt arch remains of the Water Gate piercing a thin 5m high wall along the waterfront. Of ten other towers three circular ones still remain along a 450m long stretch of the SW side high above the town (part of the wall-walk is accessible from the churchyard), and parts of the NW walls also remain. There were also two towers at the harbour entrance. At the SE end lay a small walled suburb called Base Town.

Town Walls at Youghal   *Tynte's Castle, Youghal*

OTHER CASTLE REMAINS IN COUNTY CORK

AHAKEERA W275586 11.7m long north wall remains with central fireplace above two basement loops. Higher ground to west. Belonged to O'Crowley clan.

ARDAGH W077279 Rubble mound of O'Driscoll tower on commanding rock outcrop.

BALLYBEG R552072 Rubble mound remaining of Lady Doodhaw's castle.

BALLYDELOUGHTY R752091 Wall 5m long, 4m high, 1.5m thick with battered base is only remaining part of a tower belonging to the Roches.

BALLYNACALLAGH V504411 Traces of two buildings within court 31m by 23m on islet off Dursey Island. Captured by Carew in 1602 before siege of Dunboy.

BALLYNAHOW R795029 Lowest stage (formerly vaulted) of Condon tower, now lacking east wall which contained entrance, chambers and stair.

BALLYVODANE W534810 MacCarthy tower mostly destroyed in mid 20th century. 10m long north wall still 1.5m high and defaced section of east wall.

CAHERDRINNY R798077 Footings and high NE fragment of Condon tower 12m by 10m. Entrance faced west. Second & fourth of five storeys were vaulted.

CARRIG W619994 Eastern half of round-cornered tower still two storeys high with traces of vault. Stair from south entrance leads to spiral stair in SE corner. A Roche tower repaired by Richard Gethin in the 1650s.

CARRIGANOURA R779128 North end of tower 6.2m wide on rock overlooking Funshion river. Still 8m high at NW where spiral stair began at second storey level. Entrance probably in west wall. Latrine chute at NE corner.

CARRIG COTTA W897675 Castle Mary, the Longfords' 18th-19th century ruined clifftop mansion has a partial basement which includes on the west the lowest stage of a tower, 11m by 8m, with a blocked doorway facing south.

CASTLEHAVEN W174301 Battered base only of O'Driscoll tower garrisoned by Spanish in 1601. Had gable-shaped recesses similar to nearby Raheen.

CASTLE ISLAND V959297 The west wall of an O Mahoney castle on a promontory on the north side of Castle Island stands three storeys high.

CASTLEKEVIN R623025 Stone on 19th century house on site has date 1613 and initials T.W.I. Forfeited Roche castle given to Thornhill in the 1650s.

CASTLENALACT W484609 Rubble mound marks site of O'Mahony tower set in north corner of earlier moated platform measuring 41m by 26m.

CLOGHAN W098284 O'Driscoll tower on island in Lough Hyne collapsed c1870. 10m high SW corner with traces of vault above high mound of rubble.

CLOGHANUGHERA R492203 Buried footings and fallen fragments of 2m thick wall around bawn 30m by 25m above low cliff on west side. A FitzGerald stronghold.

CLOGHGRIFFIN W439421 Rubble mound and small low fragment on ringfort edge.

CLONMEEN W404987 Walls probably of garden enclosure are only remains of house built in 1650s by the Cromwellian officer Sir Richard Kyrle.

DAVIS'S CASTLE W563840 Davis family house of uncertain date has 1m thick east wall which may be relic of castle.

DERRYVILLANE R736072 Fragment of wall with drawbar socket on east side of platform near east bank of Funshion River. Forfeited by John FitzWilliam Pigott and granted in 1588 to Arthur Hyde. Supposedly burnt in 1641.

DONEGALL V058300 Traces of O Driscoll castle on NE end of Ringarogy Island. Stones from it were taken to build the Pro-Cathedral at Skibbereen in 1826.

DONOURE W337327 Small fragment and grass-covered footings mark site of castle probably built by Barrys on tip of promontory west of Bealacoon Cove.

DOONPOWER W887595 Debris mound by causeway onto coastal promontory is all that remains of gatehouse which was rather more complete in 1914. Supposedly built by Crown in 1595 but soon captured by the Earl of Desmond and garrison executed.

DROMCARRA W289676 Very ruinous O'Leary tower, 16m by 12m, reduced to pile of rubble in 1968. Part of the NE corner stairwell can still be seen.

Dannanstown Castle

Dundareike Castle

Garryvoe Castle

Glanworth Castle

Dundareike: plan

Garryvoe: plan

Rock: plan

DUARRIGLE W250943 West end of ruined 19th century house incorporates west, north and south walls two storeys high of round cornered tower 8.6m wide. No old loops remain. An O'Keefe stronghold, supposedly destroyed during the war of 1649-52.

DUNBOGEY W728499 10m square footings of Barry tower beside rock-cut ditch on promontory above Reanies Bay. Reduced to present condition c1810.

DUNDAREIKE W300717 MacCarthy tower captured by O'Sullivan Bere in 1602. Most of it collapsed in 1833. North wall 8.5m long and stub of east wall with passage through corner carried on squinch arch at second storey level.

DUNGOURNEY W930789 12m by 14m summit of 8m high sheer-sided rock beside Dungourney river has footings of castle of branch of Barrys of Barrymore.

DUNNYCOVE W382343 Battered west wall base and pile of rubble remain of tower of O'Cowhigs on neck of promontory overlooking Dunnycove Bay.

DUNOWEN W363323 Footings and low fragment of tower 14m long and small trapezoidal bawn within coastal promontory fort.

FAHANACOWLEY W325473 15m long wall 1.3m thick and 1.5m high incorporated in field boundary may have been part of a bawn. On tree-clad clifftop site.

FARRANAMANAGH V831379 Only the lowest level remains of a tower measuring about 10m by 9m of the O'Daly clan on the shore of Dunmanus Bay.

GARRAUNIGARINAGH R794010 Only relic is two storey latrine turret on north side of lost main tower. A Condon castle which was granted in 1588 to Arthur Hyde.

GARRYCLOYNE W598799 MacCarthy tower built in 1535 later held by Travers family and then Townsends. Access to wall-walk still possible until demolition in 1949, leaving just footings about 12m square.

GARRYVOE W997688 Corner tower 4.2m square with two storeys of small vaulted rooms. SE corner with stair has fallen. Held by Carew family in late 16th century.

JOHNSTOWN R755022 20m long and 3m high wall may be part of bawn. Fragment of ogival-leaded window in modern boundary wall nearby.

KILFINNAN W229349 Much altered tower 7.7m by 6m forms SW corner of embattled 19th century mansion on shore beside Glandore Harbour.

LEAMLARA W817795 Overgrown 2m high stump of round-cornered tower 11.3m by 7.4m. Straight stair in east end wall rose from south-facing doorway.

MILLTOWN R504197 Footings of L-plan building 30m by 25. Well in middle said to mark position of kitchen. Belonged to FitzGibbon family.

RATHCOBANE W833837 Fragment of walling amid rubble mound on rock within marshland is all that remains of Barry tower said to have been dismantled in 1974.

RENNY W702993 4m high and 5m high fragment of west wall containing double-splayed loop. A FitzGerald castle later granted to Edmund Spenser.

RINGMAHON W723714 Tower 4.2m by 2.8m with two tiny upper rooms over vaulted gateway passage to former bawn. In front of house used as school.

ROCK W472389 Much altered lower two storeys of tower 7.2m wide in SW corner of farmyard. SE corner turret 3m wide projecting 2.4m contains tiny vaulted room.

ROCHFORDSTOWN W629676 Only relic of probable stronghouse is plaque on later stable with date 1630 and arms of Robert Travers and Elizabeth Boyle.

RUANE R676080 Short length of displaced walling 2m high is only relic of castle granted to Sir John Broderick c1650 after being forfeited by the Roches.

SCART W004451 Rubble mound marks site of Clan Dermot MacCarthy tower.

SHANACLOGH W760894 Three corners of Barry stronghouse with modern patching between them. NW and SE corners have projecting turrets. No old openings remain.

SHEELABOYNASKEANE'S W818891 Name recalls 17th century female outlaw leader. Two storey outbuilding is much altered stronghouse 18.5m long.

SLIEVERAGH W200777 Fragment 1.4m thick and 1.3m high and line of debris 7m to west are only remains of O'Herlihy tower on tree-clad, overgrown hillock.

TUOCUSHEEN W512621 Platform 16m square east of house has battered east retaining wall 3m high, possible relic of a Barry Oge tower or stronghouse.

WALSHESTOWN R524132 Terrace in front of 18th century house with base batter to the east and south, may represent base of castle of MacJames Barrys.

WALTERSTOWN W849683 A Barry castle. Bawn 60m by 50m with west wall 3m high with 6m wide turret projecting 2m at south end. Footings only of east and south walls.

Later buildings at KILCOR W866909 and MEADSTOWN W685618 each have a 17th century fireplace with a low stack at one end. Neither has any evidence of defences.

There may have been a MacCarthy castle at Aglish in the flooded Lee Valley.

Evidence of a MacCarthy versus O'Callaghan fight at Gortmore over supposed castle.

The tower at Donaghmore demolished c1935 was probably not a castle.

There are slight remains of mid 17th century star-shaped forts at Newtown V997492 and Rosscarbery W286363 and there was also one at Crookhaven. Others at Haulbowline Island W784655 and Carlisle W820624 are earlier, the latter being probably as early as the 1550s. CHARLES FORT of 1678-83 lies outside the period of this book.

CASTLE SITES IN COUNTY CORK

AGHADOE W000778 Sheila-na-gig came from Capel or Supple castle near house.
AGHADOWN W046331 O'Driscoll tower lay east of surviving ornamental tower.
AGHAMILLA W360426 Site of O'Hea castle on promontory beside Fealge river.
ANNAGH R4993156 Tower of MacJames Barrys demolished in 18th century.
BALLYBURDEN W585679 House & farmyard on or near site of Barrett castle.
BALLYENEHAN R722100 Site of castle marked on old maps.
BALLYHEA R550195 Replaced by Castle Harrison, itself now just humps.
BALLYHEEN R421039 Site of tower on rock above Awbeg river.
BALLYHINDON R807029 Ruin of later house on site of Roche tower.
BALLYKNOCK V943868 Derelict farm and Fitzgerald castle site within ringfort.
BALLYLEGAN R747066 Two corners of tower stood 8m high in 1907. Now gone.
BALLYMACSIMON W886901 Fitzgerald tower destroyed c1820 by treasure hunter.
BALLYMAGOOLY W591985 Site of castle on cliff above Blackwater Valley, shown on
    maps of 1589 and 1654-9, sold by Theobald Roche to James Cotter in 1682 and
    garrisoned during war of 1690. One still fragment stood in 1904.
BALLYMAPATRICK W855995 Careysville House on site of Condon tower on cliff.
BALLYNABORTAGH W699831 Site of castle SW of rectangular enclosure.
BALLYNAGERAGH R532149 Roche tower destroyed to build Castle Harrison.
BALLYOURANE W077416 Site of T-plan building shown on old OS map.
BAURGORM W032469 Site of a Clan Dermot MacCarthy tower.
BAWNLAHAN W196347 19th century house on site of stronghouse of O'Donovans.
BREGOGE R509094 No remains of Barry tower held by Philip Percival in 1640s.
BROGHILL R521244 Last remains of Desmond tower cleared away in 1950s.
BROOKLODGE W747754 Road built across site of Old Court, a Barry seat.
BURRANE W469463 Site of MacCarthy Reagh tower south of farmyard.
BURREN Downe Survey map of 1652 shows two towers in townland. Unlocated.
CAHERDUGGAN R569053 Site of Roche tower shown on map of 1654-9.
CAHERMEE R572081 Castle shown on Down Survey map of 1650s.
CARRIG R342108 Buried footings of MacAuliffe tower about 10m square.
CARRIGNANEELAGH W265677 O'Leary tower dismantled to build Kilbarry House.
CARRIGHNASSIG W565546 Site of MacCarthy Riabhach castle by Bandon river burnt
    by Captain Flower in 1600, and sacked by Captain Adderley in 1642.
CASTLE ARUNDEL W413399 Site of castle built by Lord Arundel in 13th century.
CASTLE BLAGH W721971 Site of Roche castle. Earthwork on 1842 OS map.
CASTLECOR R446067 Barry later replaced by Castlecor House, also gone.
CASTLE DOD R546160 Site 150m SE of Castle Wrixon house.
CASTLELANDS W354550 Site of Finghin MacCarthy's tower on rock outcrop.
CASTLEMEHIGAN V800261 Site of castle built in 1540 by Mehans or O'Heas.
CASTLE REDMOND W880723 Site of FitzGerald tower beside Owennacurra river.
CASTLE TERRY R772094 No remains of building shown as house on map of 1654.
CASTLETOWN V342576 Site of MacCarthy castle burnt by Cromwellians in 1651.
CASTLETREASURE W705674 Walls of castle of Gould family shown on 1842 map.
CLASHARUSHEEN W325442 Stronghouse? Chief seat of Clan Aineslis O'Donovan.
COOLAVOHER W194749 Site of O'Herlihy tower by lane in farmyard.
COOLCAUM R513172 Site of tower of FitzGibbons family.
COOLEDERA (BALLYMACODA) W886901 Farm ruins on site. Imokilly Fitzgeralds.
COOLMAIN W543436 Lower part of MacCarthy Riabhach tower 9.6m by 8.4m was
    incorporated into now-demolished house by Coolmain Bay abandoned c1870.
CORKBEG W827638 Oil refinery now occupies all of island site. Old painting shows the
    former tower and adjoining house. Part of tower collapsed in 1915.
COURTMACSHERRY W516425 Mansion on site of Robert Gookin's house & bawn.
COURTSTOWN W774718 Knoll on Little Island is site of former Barry castle.
CROOKHAVEN Remains of O'Mahony castle in middle of town mentioned in 1700.

CROSSHAVEN W799615 Site of Fitzgerald tower beside Owenabwee river.
CROWBALLY W953776 Site of castle marked as a ruin on 1842 map. White family?
CULLEN W674577 Garden of site of castle of Roche family. Ruin on 1842 map.
CURRAGH R382040 Site of MacDonagh MacCarthy tower somewhere in vicinity.
DESMOND V817282 Site of O'Mahony tower built 1495 and demolished c1850.
DONERAILE R602077 No remains of castle or of Sir William St Leger's house that
    replaced it, burnt in 1645, but occupied until 1730s. Beam found by Awbeg River
    600m to SE dated dendrochronologically to c1510 is possible relic of castle.
DROMDOWNEY R522029 Farm on site of Barry tower. Low walls remained 1905.
DROMINAGH W305985 No remains of O'Keefe tower on rock by Scarradaragh R.
DROMORE Unlocated O'Callaghan tower site somewhere in townland.
DUNBULLOGUE Unlocated site of ruined tower mentioned by Windele in 1840.
DUNEEN W387365 Farmyard on site of tower.
DUNISKY W361680 Site of MacCarthy tower on rock outcrop.
DUNMANWAY W228528 Site of 15th century MacCarthy tower demolished c1830.
DUN MIC OGHMAINN Castle site near Myross church has probably fallen into sea.
DUNNAMARK V999500 Site of castle built in 1214 by Robert Carew.
FARAHY R690105 Now gone, but lower part of tower 10m by 6m stood in 1907.
FOILDARRIG V680461 Site of Dermot MacCarthy's castle on rock near harbour.
GORTNACLOHY W128329 Site of round bawn on map of 1842. MacCarthy Reagh.
KILBEG W509565 Ditched enclosure 19m square marks site of castle.
KILCOLMAN R367001 Possibly still remained in 1920s. Site uncertain.
KILLHODENEIGUE Hodnett tower by Marino, Great Island, raided by O'Neill in 1599.
KILMACOW W982935 15th century Fitzgerald tower said to have collapsed c1745.
KINURE W698509 Site of Roche tower above Ballinaclashet creek.
KNOCKANTOTA W577867 Site of MacCarthy tower.
KNOCKMALLAVOGE W640669 Site of castle overlooking valley to west.
LEAMCON V881288 Vanished 17th century stronghouse of Sir William Hull.
LEIGHMONEY W578540 Bungalow by site of castle held by Spaniards in 1601.
LETTERTINLISH W152339 Site of O'Driscoll tower on rock outcrop.
LISHEENALEEN Unlocated site of castle shown on Downe Survey map of 1652.
LISLEE W511400 Site of probable stronghouse of Barry Roe in elevated position.
LISSAGRIFFIN V765266 Site of O'Mahony tower overlooking Barley Cove.
LISSANGLE W102398 A rock in a farmyard is the site of a Clan Dermot MacCarthy
    tower granted to the Coppingers in 1616 and later known by their name.
MARSHALSTOWN R746117 Farm on site of castle granted to Arthur Hyde in 1588.
MITCHELSTOWN R808131 Industrial complex on site of FitzGibbon tower.
NEWCASTLE W582806 Site of probable stronghouse of the Galway family.
NEWMARKET R318071 A MacAuliffe castle stood somewhere in vicinity.
OLDCOURT W852832 Supposed site of a Barrymore castle.
PHALE W334527 Site of MacCarthy tower demolished in early 19th century.
RAHANISKY W663778 Slurry pit by farm on site of tower of branch of Barrys.
RATHGOGGAN Unlocated site of castle shown on maps of c1589 and 1654-9.
RICHARDSTOWN R585073 Destroyed by storm 1865. Held by Edmund Spenser.
RINGCURRAN W654494 Charles Fort of 1678-83 lies on site of the castle.
RONAYNE'S COURT W726694 Garage on site. Fireplace of 1627 now at Blackrock.
RONAYNE'S GROVE Probable stronghouse site near Marino House, Great Island.
ROSTELLAN W869663 Site of Fitzgerald tower. Later house here demolished 1944.
SARSFIELDSCOURT W729778 Stronghouse demolished 1950s after part collapsed.
SHANAGH R661088 Site of castle of Nagles, granted to Hughes family in 1657.
SHANBALLYMORE R673068 Site of castle 200m west of house, towards river.
SHANECOURT Hodnett tower by Marino, Great Island, raided by Hugh O'Neill 1599.
SHORT W581519 Site of MacCarthy Reagh tower above Bandon river.
TEEVEENY W453173 Site of castle.
TRANTSTOWN W741818 Site of possible castle marked as ruin on 1842 map.

GAZETTEER OF CASTLES OF COUNTY KERRY

ARDEA   V774628

On a hill above the estuary of the Kenmare River are shattered and overgrown remains of walls up to 2.8m thick around the east and south sides of a court about 25m across, the other sides being protected by cliffs. There are indications of a tower at the NE corner and of another projecting from the middle of the south side. On the east side is a pointed-arched gateway. The thickness of the walls suggests a possible 13th century date. Originally an O'Moriarty seat, this castle was held by Donal Cam O'Sullivan Bear, who eventually fled to Spain after the defeat at Kinsale, and died there in 1618.

BALLINGARRY   Q759332

Overlooking the wide mouth of the Shannon are extensive but fragmentary remains of a castle held by the Cantillons from the late 13th century until their forfeiture three hundred years later for their part in the Desmond rebellion, although they seem to have remained in occupation under the new owner, George Isham. Gerard Rua Stack held the castle in 1602-3 against an attack by English combined land and sea forces. In 1641 loyal English planters led by Colonel David Crosbie withdrew into the castle, enlarged and strengthened it, built new houses, and held out against sporadic attacks by the rebel Irish until in February 1645 Sergeant James Kelly betrayed the garrison by lowering the drawbridge across the ditch which isolated the only part of the L-shaped inner ward not protected by sheer cliffs. The bases remain of the gatehouse from which the drawbridge was lowered and its abutment on the mainland, beyond which are remains Crosbie's two diverging covered ways. The inner ward contains footings of many buildings, including a probable hall and chamber in the southern part.

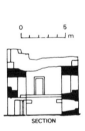

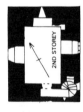

Ballinskelligs: plans

Ardea Castle

Plan of Ardea Castle

Ballingarry Castle

BALLINRUDDERY   R192184

Of the tower granted to Sir William Herbert in 1588 there remain the 2m thick and 15m high east end wall. It has fireplaces, mullion-and-transom windows, and a corner bartizan containing a chamber opening off one of the upper rooms.

BALLINSKELLIGS   V435655   A

On the shingle point at the west end of the bay is a 16th century MacCarthy tower measuring 10.1m by 7.9m standing 7m high with two unvaulted storeys. Remains of a wall-walk show that the tower never stood any higher. The pointed-arched entrance in the east wall is covered by a gunloop. The lobby is flanked by a small room on one side and a stair on the other towards a spiral stair in the SE corner. The upper room has wide embrasures in the side walls for windows once of two or three lights, and also a north facing loop.

BALLYBUNNION   Q863414   C

Part of the east wall of a tower originally about 12.7m long still stands 14.5m high (despite a recent collapse of part of it), the other walls having fallen over the cliff edge. There were four storeys, the topmost being a well-lighted room set over a vault. There are loops for two intermediate storeys and the damaged entrance doorway with a drawbar slot. The castle was destroyed in 1581.

Ballybunnion Castle

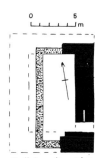

Ballybunnion: plan

Ballinskelligs Castle

Plans of Ballycarbery Castle

Ballycarbery Castle

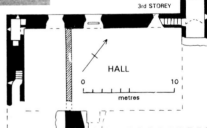

BALLYCARBERY   V447797   D

On fairly flat ground near the mouth of the Valencia River lies a 14th or 15th century hall house measuring 22.7m by 12.9m over walls up to 2.75 below vaults upon crosswalls which divide the interior into three equal compartments with lofts below the vaults. The whole SE part is missing but the rest stands almost complete with a gable set within a parapet with double-stepped battlements at the west end, and a turret (also still embattled) containing small vaulted rooms projecting at the east end of the north wall. An entrance doorway with a big drawbar slot on the north side leads into the middle compartment and a straight mural stair then leads up past a doorway to the loft over the eastern room to the NE corner. A door closed by a drawbar then impeded access before the corner could be turned and the next flight of stairs climbed in the east wall. A fine hall 12m long by 9m wide lay over the eastern and middle parts and a private chamber lay to the west. The dividing wall looks like an insertion but probably maintains an original division perhaps originally of wood. The crosswalls below are probably original since although the western one abuts awkwardly against an embrasure at ground level the layout of the openings in the north wall seems to take into account the vaults and the lofts below them. The western lofts can only have been reached by means of hatches in their floors. From the embrasure of a two-light window on the north side of the hall a murder hall commands the entrance. The private room also had a two-light north window, and probably another facing south. There is a latrine in the NW corner and a stair in the west wall descends below it to end high up in the side of a window embrasure in the cellar below. There was a door at the bottom and the drop was accessed by a wooden ladder or steps that could be removed if greater security was needed. At a distance of 7.4m away from the hall house are two sides of a later bawn wall 1.5m thick pierced on the west and NW with several loops. A gateway can be traced on the north side. This was an important seat of MacCarthy Mor occupied by the O'Connells as hereditary wardens. In the 1590s it was granted to Sir Valentine Browne. It was re-occupied by the MacCarthys during the wars of the 1640s and was slighted by the Cromwellians in 1651-2. See page 9.

BALLYCARNAHAN   V549589   C

South of Caherdaniel is the lower part of a 16th century tower with two unvaulted storeys now remaining. It measures 10.5 by 8.2m over walls 1.4m thick, except that the NE is thicker so as to contain the entrance with a chamber on one side and a spiral stair in the north corner, and there was another chamber above on the second storey. A gunloop off the foot of the stair commands the entrance. Each room contains a loop in each of the other three walls.

BALLYMALIS   V840938   A

This tower by the east bank of the Laune was probably built by the O'Moriartys or Murrays c1600. It was confiscated in 1677 and granted to Sir Francis Brewster, from whom it passed to Alexander Eager. The tower measures 14.8m by 9.6m over battered walls 1.9m thick ant the sides. The 4m thick east wall contains the entrance and a guard room and then has a mural chamber on each of the unvaulted upper three levels, although the topmost chamber is now undivided from the main room. At third storey level passages off the NE and SW corners of the main room lead to triangular chambers with machicolations and gunloops in bartizans on the outer corners. Off the passage to the SW bartizan room is a latrine. The second and third storeys have fireplaces in the west end wall and the top room has a fireplace on the north side. This room has on either side near the west end a pair of windows of three lights with ogival heads with transoms and square hoodmoulds. There are two light windows further east and others on the third storey.

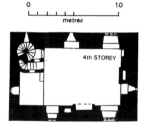

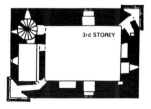

Ballymalis: plans

Ballymalis Castle

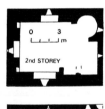

Ballycarnahan: plans

Ballycarnahan Castle

Barrow Castle (& Fenit Castle in background)

Ballymaquim Castle

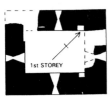

Plans of Ballymaquim Castle

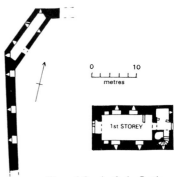

Plan of Carrigafoyle Castle

BALLYMAQUIM   Q829264   D

There are double-splayed loops in the lowest level of this tower, which measures 11.2m by 9m over walls 2.2m thick and has a vault over the third storey, where there is a passage in the SE wall. The second storey has a fireplace between two rooms in the NE wall, and there is a chamber in the NW haunch of the vault. No stair remains as a result of the loss of the west corner, but part of the NW-facing entrance survives here.

BARROW or ROUND CASTLE   Q725184

On the shore by the entrance to the harbour lies a 6m high circular tower 11.5m in diameter containing two levels of almost rectangular rooms linked by a spiral stair beside the east facing entrance which has a pointed head and a chain-hole in the jamb. Originally there were probably two upper storeys. The castle was built by the de Clahulls but was held by the Denny family in the late 17th century. It is thought that a chain was extended across the harbour to the tower on Fenit Island.

CAPPANACUSH   V835692

Lying within woodland is the 10.5m long south wall of a tower probably built c1440 by Conchur O'Sullivan. There is evidence of a vault over the third storey, and that the east wall contained mural chambers and the entrance, with a stair probably in the NE corner.

CARRIGAFOYLE Q986475 B

This fine tower partly standing 23m high lies on the shore of Ballylongford Bay. It was built c1500 by the chief of the O'Conors of Kerry. In March 1580 the Italian engineer Captain Julian with 15 Irish and 16 Spaniards held the castle for the Earl of Desmond against an English force led by Sir William Pelham. The attackers brought up artillery by sea, battered down the landward side of the bawn and stormed the castle within two days. Those within were hanged and Pelham sent the Earl of Desmond's plate, which was in the castle, to Queen Elizabeth. During the rebellion of O'Neill the O'Conors recovered their castle, although they were forced to surrender it to Sir George Carew in 1600, and it was then granted to Sir Charles Wilmot. The castle was finally wrecked during the war of 1649-52.

The tower is built of small stones neatly layered. It was surrounded by an inner bawn with round turrets, now destroyed, with a dock for boats between it and an outer bawn on the landward side, the loopholed 2m thick west wall of which survives, with a chamber in the chamfered-off NW corner. The tower is now only reached from the landward side because of the collapse of the upper parts at this end. Originally the only entrance lay in the 4.6m thick facing the sea. The other walls are 2.2m thick, the overall dimensions being 17.9m by 9.7m. The thick walls has the usual arrangement of a spiral stair off one side of the entrance passage, and a guard room on the other with a tier of mural rooms (here as large as 5m by 3.3m) above. There is an oven at the base of the stair and the ground floor room was long enough to need two loops on each long side. Above was a loft and at this level a passage is screened off to give access from the stair to a latrine in the far side wall. There were three move levels above with a vault below the topmost room.

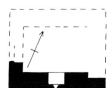

Cappanacush: plan

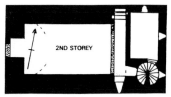

Carrigafoyle: plan of tower

0   10
metres

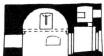

Barrow: plans & section

Carrigafoyle Castle

CASTLE CONWAY   V776966

A castle built here at Killorglin by Maurice Fitz-Gerald in 1215 was burnt by the MacCarthys in 1261 and 1280, but later replaced by a tower house of which the south wall 14.5m long still stands two storeys high. It has a SW corner stair turret beside a mostly-buried entrance doorway and adjoins 19th century buildings, the interior now being a garden. The second storey has a latrine opening off the staircase. The building is now named after Captain Jenkin Conway, who rebuilt the tower forfeited by the MacCarthys in 1583 and provided it with a bawn. Florence MacCarthy burnt it in 1600 and it was described as ruinous in 1682, but it was repaired and remained inhabited for fifty years after it passed out of the hands of the Conway-Blennerhasset family in 1795.

CASTLE CORE   V850917   D

This castle belonged to the Macgillycuddys (a branch of the O'Sullivans), one of whom, Donough, is said to have burnt the tower when he was forfeited for his part in the wars of the 1640s. The north end wall remains with fireplaces on the first, second and fourth storeys of a tower 10.2m wide with a wall-walk 14.5m above ground. The parapet is corbelled out behind a gable with chimney-stacks and has a square bartizan with a chamfered off NW outer corner and gunloops.

CASTLE COVE or BUNANEER   V593602

This castle built either by O'Sullivan Mor or the Brennans measuring 11.5m by 10m now stands two storeys high, but most of the south end wall has fallen. The west wall contained two mural chambers, one of which has a murder-hole over the entrance. There is a spiral stair in the NW corner. The main upper room has a fireplace, beside which is a chute from a latrine higher up. The upper walls had recessed centres as at Raheen in Cork.

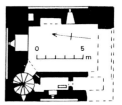

Castle Cove: plan

Castle Island

Castle Core

CASTLE ISLAND Q999096 B

Hidden away from the main street behind some houses are the lower part of a bawn corner tower about 8.5m by 6.5m with part of a vault and double splayed loop, and 60m away to the NE is a lofty fragment of a 4m square corner turret of a tower house which may have had a similar plan to that at Listowell. In 1600 Carew described the castle as having been the chief seat of the Earl of Desmond. See page 103.

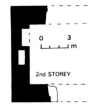

Castle Core: plan

CASTLE LOUGH V971882 G

Set on a low promontory (once an island) in Lough Leane, and now an ornament in the grounds of an hotel, are the lower parts of a MacCarthy castle captured by Ludlow in 1652. It consisted of a main block about 8m wide now lacking its southern half. Rather more remains of a northerly extension containing a vaulted room and a NE wing containing a chute for several latrines.

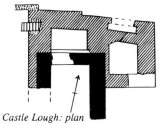

Castle Lough: plan

CASTLEMAINE Q835031

Upon the middle arches of the four-arch bridge stood a Desmond castle which was captured in 1510 by the Earl of Kildare. It was surrendered to Sir John Perrot after being bombardment for eleven weeks in 1571, but in 1573 was recaptured by James Fitz-Maurice by means of a stratagem. In 1583 the head of the Earl of Desmond was brought here for public display. The Sugan Earl of Desmond besieged the castle in 1598 and finally took it in 1599. It was captured by the Confederate Irish in 1641 and is thought to have been demolished by the Cromwellians, although ruins of it remain until the 18th century.

DINGLE Q445012

On the west side of the town are fragments of walls for which murage was granted in the 13th and 14th centuries, the area enclosed being a modest 350m by 180m. The Husseys tower of c1580 used in 1815 as the town prison probably lay on the SW side. The tower of the Rice family once dated 1586 stood at the junction of Green Street and Main Street, and a third tower once held by the Knight of Kerry lay near the north end of Main Street.

Fieries Castle

Castle Lough

Dunkerron: plans

Dunkerron Castle

DUNKERRON   V884705

This tower measuring 11.5m by 10.5m over walls up to 2.6m thick with double-splayed loops in the lowest level lies in the grounds of the house. The SE corner, now broken down, contained a spiral stair, and there are latrines in the NE corner. The north wall stands 18m high and there are traces of a former vault over the second of four storeys. A wing 4.7m wide projects 3.8m from the west end of the south wall so as to flank the entrance, the wing lowest level being a prison and having a fragment of a bawn wall extending south from it. Further east, forming part of the bawn but also part of a house built in the 1590s by Owen O'Sullivan and his second wife Sily MacCarthy, is a 12m long and 1.2m thick fragment with three loops and an upper fireplace. One of four carved stones, now missing bore the date 1596 and their names. Dunkerron remained the chief O'Sullivan Mor seat until it was confiscated in 1656 and given to Sir William Petty.

DUNLOE   V884912   G

A promontory in the grounds of the hotel is the likely site of Maurice FitzGerald's castle of 1215, burnt by the MacCarthys in 1261 and 1280. By the ditch cutting it off is a 2m high fragment of walling of uncertain date. Further east stands a derelict four storey O'Sullivan tower probably dating from just after an older tower was destroyed by the Earl of Ormond in 1570. After the forfeiture of the O'Sullivans in 1656 the castle went to Sir William Petty but by 1700 it had passed to the O'Mahonys, one of whom in the 1820s rebuilt the east wall with brick ogival-headed windows. The north-facing entrance has been blocked up. The tower originally measured 11.3m by 8m over walls up to 1.8m thick. The west wall contains two inserted and blocked upper fireplaces, one of which blocks a mural staircase, whilst the second storey has a fireplace in the south wall. Hidden in ivy at the top are a machicolation facing west and a SW corner bartizan.

Dunloe Castle

Ferriter's Castle

FENIT   Q723179

There may have been a chain extended across Barrow Harbour from the circular tower on the east side to the rectangular tower 10m by 8.7m over walls 2.2m thick on the opposite shore of Fenit Island. There are upper and lower doorways facing seawards. The SE corner is destroyed but the rest stands 18m high. See background of Barrow photo, page 98.

FERRITER'S   V322054   G

Only the west corner still stands of a tower built by the Ferriter family c1460. The corner is chamfered off. There were probably four storeys with the second vaulted. The base of the east corner also remains, with a latrine chute, and indicating that the tower measured 9.8m by 8.3m over walls 1.5m thick. The poet-scholar Piaras Ferriter was the last of the native Irish chiefs to submit to Cromwell. His safe conduct was dishonoured by his hanging at Martyrs' Hill at Killarney in 1653.

FIERIES   Q906023

Hidden under ivy on a rock behind a house is the lower part of a tower 9.7m wide over walls 2.1m thick, probably once 14m long, although the outer part of the thick east end wall containing a tier of chambers over the entrance has been destroyed by quarrying away the rock supporting it. The lofty basement still retaining half of its vault is now entered through a former loop embrasure on the south side. See page 101.

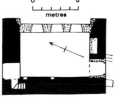

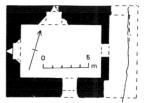

Dunloe: plan   *Castle Island: plan*   *Ferriter's: plan*   *Fieries: plan*

GALLARUS   Q388054   D

Not far north of the famous Gallarus oratory on the Dingle peninsular is a 16th century tower built by the Knight of Kerry. It contains four storeys under a vault, above which there was originally a fifth storey. At the foot of the steeply battered walls the tower measures 10.6m by 8.7m with the west and north walls 1.8m thick, but the north and east walls made thick to accommodate mural chambers. The north facing entrance has a drawbar slot. There are no surviving stairs between the lower levels. One mutilated loop on the west side retains an ogival head. Two basement loops are double splayed. There appears to have been a latrine on the second storey.

KILLAGHA   V048860

This 18m high O'Donohue tower where the poet-chief Geoffrey gave his famous feasts measures 15.6m by 11m over walls up to 2.4m thick. The five main rooms connected by a stair in the destroyed NE corner were without vaults, the only vaulting being over the guard-room beside the entrance in the east end wall rising higher than the rest. There are chimneys on the west and south walls for upper storey fireplaces. A bartizan at third storey level has been mostly destroyed.

KILMURRY   R057096   D

A wing 7.2m wide containing the entrance and presumably also a vanished timber staircase projects 6.7m from the SE side of a main block 20m by 12m over walls 2.8m thick having many gunloops in the lowest level, where there is a kitchen fireplace at the NE end. The second storey seems to have been subdivided into a main hall with a fireplace on the NW side and a private room at the NE end with its own fireplace and a latrine with an angle loop in the east corner. The third storey was also subdivided and had a room in a destroyed bartizan on the south corner, whilst there was a bartizan at wall-walk level upon the west corner. The castle belonged to the FitzGeralds.

LECK   Q861450   C

A 10m high headland isolated by a narrow natural cleft descending to sea level bears fragments of a D-shaped bawn about 30m across. In the SE corner is the three storey high south wall of a tower about 9m wide. This FitzGerald castle had been dismantled by 1641, when it was granted to Trinity College, Dublin. See front cover picture.

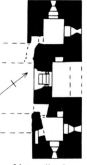

Listowell: plan

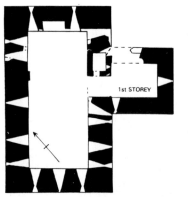

1st STOREY

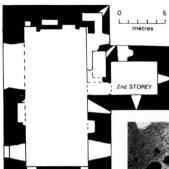

2nd STOREY

0   5
metres

Plans of Kilmurry Castle

Fireplace at Kilmurry

Gallarus Castle

Listowell Castle

LISTOWELL   Q989335   B

Just off the town square is one end wall of a castle of the MacGilligans. This wall formed part of a castle like Bunratty in County Clare with square turrets at all four corners of an rectangular main building 9.5m wide over walls 2m thick. As at Bunratty the two surviving turrets, each measuring 6.5m by 6m, are joined at the top by an arch. They contain rooms with double-splayed loops.

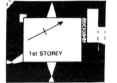

Gallarus: plans

Kilmurry Castle

Killagha Castle

LIXNAW   V855347   D

Shapeless ivy-covered walls remain of The Court, an unfortified 17th century mansion with a main east range 43m long and a north range around an inner court, and an outer court or walled garden to the east. It was enlarged in the 18th century but was a ruin by 1837. Further east only a platform about 40m across with a ditch and traces of outworks and a 5m diameter building called the Cockhouse remains of castle of the Knight of Kerry. Here in 1568 Thomas Fitz-Maurice routed James Fitz-Maurice Fitz-Gerald. In 1600 Sir Charles Wilmot occupied the castle before the Fitz-Maurices could destroy it. It was returned to Thomas Fitz-Maurice in 1601 but after Spanish troops arrived at Kinsale he rebelled again and Wilmot had to capture the castle again in 1602.

MINARD   V554992   A

This 15th century tower of the Knight of Kerry blown up by the Cromwellians in 1650 lies on a hillock above a small stream on the south side of the Dingle peninsular. It measures 15.1m by 11.8m at the base of the battered and neatly faced walls which are are 2.5m to 3.3m thick. The lowest level has loops with external splays in three walls, and an entrance passage facing west with two separate sets of rebates and drawbar slots. There was probably a second storey upper entrance as the spiral stair in the SE corner only began at that level. The main room at that level had a window on each side and a fireplace on the north side. The SW corner contains a chamber 5.4m long by 1.8m wide and there was in the NE corner a smaller chamber, perhaps with a latrine, reached from the now mostly destroyed eastern window embrasure. The third storey was vaulted and has a mural chamber in the NW corner with the rare feature of a two-light window set on the angle, with the mullion forming the corner of the building. Originally there was at least one further storey above the vault.

PALLIS   V884932

The chief seat of MacCarthy Mor, this castle destroyed in 1837 stood close to the ringfort north of Beaufort Bridge. It was captured in 1510 by the Earl of Kildare acting as Lord Deputy. In 1596 the heiress of the then chief defied both her father and the English government by eloping from the castle with Finghin MacCarthy Reagh, marrying him at night in the then derelict Muckross Friary on the other side of Lough Leane. Finghin was imprisoned in the Tower of London for this.

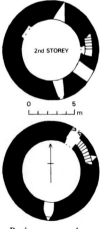

Parkavonear Castle

Parkavonear: plans

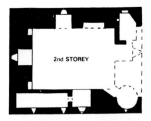

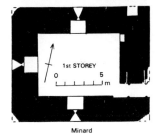

Minard

Minard Castle

Rahoneen Castle: plans

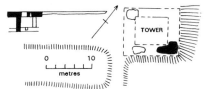

Plan of Pookeenee Castle

PARKAVONEAR   V934926   A

In a field SW of Aghadoe cathedral is a round tower 10.6m in diameter over walls 2.1m thick. It is a plain building just 7m high containing two storeys standing in the middle of a square enclosure with south corner bastions which once had a curtain wall and moat. It may be a native Irish version of an early 13th century Norman round keep. The entrance at ground level leads into a cellar with just one narrow loop. From one side of the passage a stair curves round in the walling to terminate at the upper storey without any sign of a further stair to any upper storeys or battlements. The upper room has a shallow fireplace, two narrow loops and a wider opening, probably once a two light window.

POOKEENEE   Q861419

On the south side of Doon Cove, just north of Ballybunnion, is a large promontory fort with slight traces of later stone defences on the inside edge of the ditch. At the east end are fragments of a tower house measuring about 12m by 10.5m over walls 2.5m thick. A wall ran west from it to a small chamber 19.6m to the west.

RAHONEEN   Q759201   D

The east end of a tower 9m by 8m stands two storeys high. A service stair in the south wall begins at a level well above that of the cellar floor, whilst the spiral stair in the NE corner started at the level of the entrance set just below the floor of the room over the vault, which has a ruinous latrine in the SE corner.

Reencaheragh Castle

Rahoneen Castle

Rathsinnane Castle

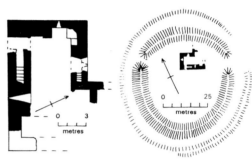

Plans of Rathsinnane Castle

RATHSINNANE   Q369017   A

This tower built by the Knight of Kerry to command the pass between Ballyferiter and Ventry on the Dingle peninsular lies within an impressive ringfort 45m across with a very steeply sided rampart rising up to 7m above the surrounding ditch. The castle was captured by Sir Charles Wilmot in 1602 and destroyed during the Cromwellian period. The tower had a main block 13.9m by 8.6m with a wing about 7.4m wide projecting from the eastern half of the north side. The wing has been destroyed along with the eastern end of the main block, which appears to have contained a tier of mural chambers. Unusually, the entrance lay elsewhere, being near the west end of the south wall, in which a straight stair leads up. The second storey was vaulted and the third storey has thinner walls brought back to a sufficient thickness to carry a wall-walk by the provision of internal arcading.

REENCAHERAGH   V340722

A headland on the mainland almost opposite Bray Head on Valencia Island is closed off by the lower part of a wall 1.5m thick and 34m long, with part of a thinner return wall at the east end. Towards this end lies a rectangular gatehouse, probably 16th century. It measures 6.7m by 4.5m and has small rooms on either side of a passage which was arched over with huge slabs, the inner archway having a drawbar slot securing a door against the internal defended area, within which the building entirely projects. There is a stair in the west end wall. There is a postern in the curtain wall just west of the gatehouse. About 14m behind the gatehouse lie foundations of a building 11.5m long, by 6.5m with doorways opposite each other near the west ends of each side wall.

ROSS   V949887   E

This famous and often illustrated building lies on a promontory in Lough Leane. It consists of a tower house 13m long with a greatest width of 9.6m lying with a bawn wall with circular NW and NE corner flankers protecting its north and east sides. Recently restored by the Irish Office of Works, having been taken into state care in 1970, the tower house contains a vaulted basement, second and third storeys with mural chambers over the entrance in the north end wall, and a fourth storey hall over a second vault. The third storey has an angle loop and a long passage to a latrine in the NW corner. The presence of gunloops commanding the entrance and what appear to be original fireplaces in the second and fourth storeys suggest an early 16th century date, whilst the three light windows of the hall are later insertions. This level now has a screen dividing off a service area at the north end beside the spiral stair in the NE corner. This corner rises above the main wall-walk, which has square bartizans with gunloops at the NW and SE corners. The castle formed the chief seat of O'Donoghue Mor until it was acquired by MacCarthy Mor after the Desmond Rebellion. Soon afterwards it was mortgaged to Sir Valentine Browne, who eventually took possession and whose descendants held it until the death in 1956 of the seventh Earl of Kenmare, a title conferred on them by James II. In 1652 Lord Muskerry held the castle against a Cromwellian force of 1,500 foot and 700 horse led by Ludlow. It was surrendered after floating batteries were brought up to bombard it from the lough, thus fulfilling an ancient tradition that the castle would remain impregnable until attacked from the water. The south end of the bawn was later replaced by a three storey block extending from the tower with a more spacious bawn platform to the east with a SE bastion. Here were stationed two companies of infantry until 1825.

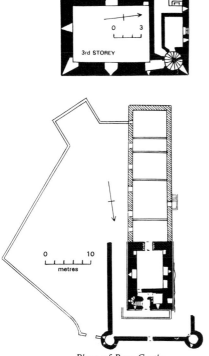

3rd STOREY

Plans of Ross Castle

Ross Castle

Listowell Castle

2nd STOREY

Old postcard of Ross Castle

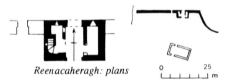

Reenacaheragh: plans

0   25
└┴┴┴┴┴┘ m

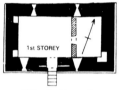

1st STOREY

Bealagrellagh: plan   *Kilmakeddar: plan*

SMERWICK   Q348071

On a cliff-edge SE of Smerwick, on the west side of the bay near the end of the Dingle peninsular is a fort called Dun an Oir which was built by a party of Italians and Spaniards led by James MitzMaurice, who landed in the bay in September 1580. Lord Deputy Grey and Admiral Winter attacked the fort seven weeks later and after a three day bombardment the garrison surrendered. The officers were spared but about 600 common soldiers and 17 Irish men and women were massacred. Father Laurence Moore, Oliver Plunket, and a Catholic Englishman, William Wollick, were also captured, and, refusing to acknowledge the religious supremacy of Elizabeth I, were savagely tortured and mutilated before being hanged. The remains of the fort comprise an outer court 45m by 15m with two south facing bastions (the western one destroyed) on the mainland and a cliff-top inner court about 23m by 45m isolated on the south side by a rock-cut ditch. It all seems rather small to have accommodated over 600 people.

TRALEE   Q834145

Castle Street is named after one of the chief seats of the Earls of Desmond, thirteen of whom were buried in the church of the nearby Dominican friary. The town and castle both suffered much damage during the rebellion of the 15th Earl, and were subsequently granted to Sir Edward Denny. In 1641 they were captured by a Confederate Catholic force under Sir Piaras Ferriter but in 1643 they were captured by Murrough O'Brien (known as The Burner) after he changed sides. The town was burnt by Jacobites in 1691 when they retired in the face of a bigger Williamite army. Part of an urban tower house called Castle MacEllistrom lay in Pembroke Street until 1838, and there was once a another urban tower house in Denny Street.

OTHER CASTLE REMAINS IN COUNTY KERRY

BALLYBEGGAN Q863155 Fragmentary Hussey family tower near Tralee racecouse. Measures 13m by 10m with stair in SE corner and traces of third storey vault.

BALLYPLYMOTH R038096 Four storey high NE corner and lower parts of adjoining walls of FitzGerald tower later given to the Herberts. See page 8.

BEALAGRELLAGH Q898111 North end of 8.6m wide MacElliot tower mostly demolished in 1926. Two loops and traces of a vault remain.

BEAUFORT V882923 18th century house may stand on foundations of tower built in 1640s by Captain Sullivan known as Short Castle.

CASTLE QUARTER or BEAL Q909484 Ditched platform roughly 60m square said to have once had a stone wall.

CLASHMELCON Q815367 2.5m high and 1.7m thick fragment of east wall of tower built by Brown family. Traces of spiral staircase. Set on inside edge of ditch cutting off coastal promontory 35m wide. See photo on page 7.

CLOONMEALAUN Q889041 6m high NE corner of a MacCarthy tower.

FERMOYLE V452707 14m long south wall 1.4m thick, still partly 6m high, of an O'Sullivan tower with vaulted chamber in SE corner, probably a guardroom beside an east-facing entrance.

KILMAKEDDAR V401059 Two storey hall-house for priest of adjacent church. Measures 11.8m by 7.2m over walls 1.5m thick with double-splayed loops in lowest level. Inserted cross-wall. South facing doorway at ground level has a drawbar slot.

LOUGH CURRANE V517649 Remains of structure (possibly unmortared) 21m square, up to 1.5m high with walls 2m thick now below surface of lough.

MOLAHIFFE Q911046 Shapeless, ivy-clad tall fragment of tower.

RATHMORREL Q796300 Pile of rubble of De Cantillon castle beside house.

OTHER CASTLE SITES IN COUNTY KERRY

ARABELLA Q911120 The footings may still remain of a tower here.

ARDFERT Q787211 East of cathedral is site of castle built by Knight of Kerry on site of earlier castle of 1311. Besieged by Desmonds 1580 and 1583. Captured in 1600 by Sir Charles Wilmot, who then hanged the constable.

ASTEE WEST Last remains of the castle were cleared away about fifty years ago.

BALLINEANIG Q358056 Site of Ferriters tower 9.8m by 7.2m with SW corner stair.

CARRIGCLAUREAGH Q861450 Site of Fitz-Gerald castle on headland.

CASTLE GREGORY Q621134 Village named after vanished 16th century castle of Gregory Hoare. Captured by Cromwellians in 1649-52. Gone by 1841.

CASTLE DRUM Q793037 Only a pile of rubble remains of a Moriarty castle demolished in 1641.

GLANDINE Q704083 Site of castle held in 1610 by Edmund Fitz-John.

KNOCKANUSH Q789161 Motte and bailey earthworks still remain, but no masonry.

LISCAHANE Q793193 Circular earthwork on site of castle granted by Elizabeth I in 1587 to Sir Francis Walsingham and Edward Dunne

MACCROHAN'S V474770 Ditched platform 30m square on site of castle named after a branch of the O'Sullivans.

SHORT V532795 Platform 18m by 14m marks site of MacCarthy castle.

OTHER CASTLE SITES: Ahalane (unlocated), Ardtully Q986729, Ballingolin (unlocated), Ballingowan Q869136, Ballykealy Q788271, Ballymacadam R028102, Caheratranny (unlocated), Camp Q699192, Carrignafeela Q905150, Castleshannon (unlocated), Castleview Q999096, Cordal Q065082, Doon East (unlocated), Fermoyle Q546120, Flesk V986898, Glanappa (unlocated), Great Blasket V279979, Inch (unlocated), Litter (unlocated), Meanus Q937061, Meenagohane (unlocated), Moorestown Q403098, Tarbert & Tarbert East (both unlocated), Tooreen Q957147.

GAZETTEER OF WATERFORD CASTLES

ARDMORE   X189774

A platform NE of the cathedral is the likely site of a tower and bawn originally owned by the Mernin family. It was briefly occupied by the Yorkist pretender Perkin Warbeck in 1496 and in the 1580s it went to Sir Walter Raleigh. It was granted to Sir John Dowdall in 1593 and later passed to Sir Edward Harris. By 1642, when Lord Dungarvan and Lord Broghill captured the castle and killed over 100 of the Catholic defenders, it was in the hands of the Bishop of Ardmore.

BALLYCANVAN   S661110

The ruined later house above the River Suir incorporates a much altered tower measuring 7.8m by 6.5m with evidence of three storeys. The east wall contains the entrance with a mural chamber above and a blocked mural staircase.

BALLYCLOHY   S322211   D

On the south side of an enclosure 53m by 40 defined by a slight scarp and traces of a ditch is a 16th century circular tower 8.8m in diameter which was owned by John Butler in 1640. The northern part containing the entrance and the eastern part containing stairs have fallen but the south and west part still stand 10m high. There are three storeys of rectangular rooms with the topmost set above remains of a vault and having a fireplace. The second storey has a latrine and both the first and second storey have window embrasures fitted with gunloops.

BALLYDUFF   X968989   D

This stronghouse of three storeys and an attic with several upper windows of three and four lights with hoodmoulds was built in 1627 for Richard Boyle, Earl of Cork. It measures 15m by 9.4m and had the south and north walls flanked by gunloops in a stairs wing and an entrance wing. The latter faces a bawn 13.4m square enclosed by walls 0.8m thick with flankers 4.7m square set at the northern corners so that they also flank the end walls of the house in which there are fireplaces. The bawn and the NE flanker are rather obscured by modern farm buildings.

Ballycloghy Castle

Ballycanvan Castle

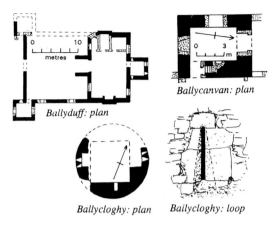

Ballyduff: plan

Ballycanvan: plan

Ballycloghy: plan   *Ballycloghy: loop*

Ballyduff Castle

BALLYGUNNER   S645089

This still-occupied three storey late 16th century house with five chimney stacks measures 15.5m by 8m. Three windows with pairs of round-headed lights survived 19th century remodelling. In 1640 it was a ruin in the possession of James Walsh of Little Island.

BALLYMACLODE   S656100

In a farmyard are the lowest two storeys of a tower measuring 10m by 8.3m which was held by Lord Power of Curraghmore in 1640. The west wall contains a entrance which was protected by a murder hole from a level above the surviving vault. The stair is covered by a gunloop from the second storey room. This room has no doorway off the stair and was reached by a hatch from below. It has an ogival-headed window and fireplace on the north, a latrine (now blocked) at the SE corner, a western mural room containing a murder hole, and also once had a timber gallery around the south, east and west sides.

BUTLERSTOWN   S558088

This tower on a rock outcrop was built by the Nugents sometime after they obtained the estate by marriage to a Butler heiress. The Sherlocks bought the tower in 1544 and held it until it was sold in the early 19th century to the Backas family. They restored the tower, which had been damaged by fire in 1794, providing a new parapet and turrets, new windows, and adding a new house against the west wall. The tower measures 12.2m by 10.2m and has an entrance in the south end wall, which contains mural chambers and a latrine at second storey level, where the main room is vaulted and has a mural passage on the west and north sides. Another latrine further up has been destroyed. The stair in the SW corner no longer connects with the lowest storey.

CAPPAGH   X181966

A turret projects at the NW corner of a FitzGerald tower measuring 9m by 8m lying in woods. The north wall has a fireplace higher up. There are traces of a bawn to the south.

CASTLEQUARTER   S174011

High above the Finisk River is an early 16th century MacGrath tower now reduced and modernised as a dwelling of two storeys and an attic. It was held by Garret FitzGerald of Dromana in 1640. It measures 10m by 8m and has an entrance and mural stairs (not in use) in the north wall. The NE corner contains a spiral stair up from the second storey.

Cloncoskoran Castle

Clonea Castle

CLONCOSKORAN   X297954   C

This tower was held by Richard Nugent in the 1640s and was later held by the Nugent-Humbles, but it was probably built by the Shanahans. The northern half still partly stands four storeys high with evidence of a SW corner spiral stair linking the upper levels. The second storey had a vault and one window with embrasure seats.

CLONEA   S384134   C

This tower lies on a rock outcrop surrounded by a ditch and to the north are buried footings of a wall 0.9m thick with two flanking turrets surrounding a bawn 30m square. The tower measures 14.5m by 11.1m and had an entrance in the south wall, most of which has collapsed, along with much of the west wall and the corner between them. A spiral stair lay in the SE corner. The third storey lay over a vault and both it and the vaulted loft above it had mural chambers in the west and south walls. The fifth storey also had an east mural chamber, and there was a sixth storey attic room. The castle belonged to Lord Power c1640 when it was "out of repair". See page 3.

COOLNAMUCK   S366214   D

The south end wall of a 16th century tower 9.2m wide over walls 1.7m thick still stands to full height with evidence of a vaulted ground floor room with gunloops in the surviving window embrasure, three upper storeys, the topmost having a fireplace, and a circular bartizan on the SE corner, set over where the wall-walks passed through chambers in the south wall. The tower lies within a bawn 54m square with the wall still 4m high on the east, where they lies above a steep slope. The north side is missing and only the base remains of a circular flanker 4.8m in diameter at the NE corner, but the slightly smaller NW flanker still has two storeys, both with gunloops. A stone bearing the date 1588 and the initials of its likely builder Geraldus Wall was removed in the 19th century.

CULLEN   S566043   C

On a rock is a tower measuring 9.7m by 8.7m with a damaged entrance on the east side. The lowest level had a fireplace on the south and a latrine with an angle loop in the NW corner. The second storey reached by a mural stair on the east had a latrine on the north and angle loops to the SE and SW. Nothing remains of any upper levels and there are no vaults. It was possibly held by Francis Bryver in 1640.

DERRINLAUR   S251227   D

This castle is first mentioned in 1520 when possession was in dispute between the Powers and Butlers. It was captured by John FitzGerald, Earl of Desmond in 1574 but his garrison was massacred after the castle was recaptured by the Viceroy Sir William FitzWilliam. Standing at the NE corner of a later block 12m by 9m of which all that survives is a low corner tower 7.4m in diameter at the SE corner, is a tower, circular both in and out at each of four storeys, measuring 11m in diameter over walls 2.8m thick, partly still standing 15m high with a machicolation at the top.

DROMANA   X092951

This seat of the FitzGerald lords of Decies was held by the Villier-Stuarts in the 18th and 19th centuries. Buildings of the Villier-Stuart period have gone, leaving the lower part of a tower house with one window with twin ogival-headed lights with decorated spandrels and a hoodmoulding within a late 17th century two storey house of eight bays. There is also an earlier round tower 12m in diameter, perhaps 13th century, and a short length of adjacent coeval walling, both 6m high.

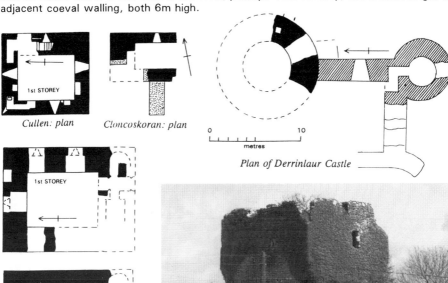

Cullen: plan

Cloncoskoran: plan

0   10
metres

Plan of Derrinlaur Castle

1st STOREY

1st STOREY

2nd STOREY

Clonea; plans

Cullen Castle

DUNGARVAN   X263931   C

King John had a castle here by 1215, and the twelve-sided shell keep 20m in diameter internally may be of that period. It envelops a motte in the same way as the English 12th century shell keeps at Berkeley and Farnham and has a gateway facing NE. On the north and south the wall is now broken down to motte summit level and replaced by thin modern walls above. Set into the mound on the north is a large vaulted chamber later adapted with gunports as a battery facing out to sea. Above it there was originally just one upper room but a second storey was created later. Another large two storey building once lay on the higher ground filling the southern part of the keep.

The keep lies mostly within the west end of a bailey 50m long by 30m wide with an 11m high round tower 10.5m in diameter at the SW corner and a gatehouse at the SE corner comprising a passage with a portcullis groove and flanked by two U-shaped towers 6m wide and 9m long, now mostly reduced to their lower storey. On the northern side, facing the sea, the curtain has been replaced by a thin modern wall. The round tower has three storeys linked by a spiral stair, the lowest room having an inserted vault partly blocking the arrowloops of the second storey, whilst the third storey has a fireplace. The bailey defences date from c1260-75, when work on the castle is recorded. The FitzGeralds had possession of it from 1285 until 1535 when it was captured by Lord Deputy Skeffington after the wall was breached with artillery. It was then retained by the Earl of Ossory until the Crown assumed direct control in 1543. The parapet on the 5m high curtain was subsequently equipped with gunloops and, as revealed by excavations in 1997, a new tower was built in the bailey NE corner to replace a destroyed original rectangular tower there. The castle was captured and recaptured several times in the wars of the 1640s and was taken by Cromwell in 1650. A new barracks built inside the bailey in the 1740s was used as a police station until 1987, since when extensive renovations have been carried out.

The castle lay near the NE corner of the town walls, which seem to have been rebuilt in the 1620s, when Richard Boyle, Earl of Cork had control of Dungarvan. There are no remains of the walls, although recent excavations have revealed traces of them in three places, nor does anything remain of the west, south, or east gates. The town was captured by the Confederates in 1642 but was recaptured later that year by William St Leger. The Confederates took it again in 1645 and held it until it was captured by Cromwell's forces in 1649.

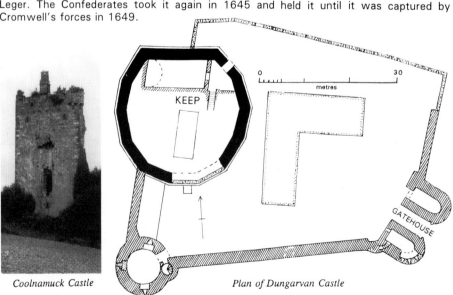

Coolnamuck Castle   *Plan of Dungarvan Castle*

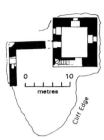

Plan of Dunhill Castle

Back of gatehouse at Dungarvan

At S268930, beside the vanished Augustinian abbey of Dungarvan, there stood a tower house known as MacGrath's Castle, which collapsed in 1916. It measured about 11.5m by 9.5m and is said to have had six storeys and an accompanying bawn.

DUNHILL   S505008   C

Dramatically placed on a rock above the Annestown stream is a tower 10.5m by 9.6m projecting from the NW corner of a tiny shovel-shaped bawn just 19m by 12m and thus protecting the bawn gateway south of it. There are low sections of walling 1.5m thick on the more accessible west and south sides of the bawn, the latter having a window embrasure with seats indicating a former building. The tower has a doorway and stair in the east wall. The second storey is vaulted and has a mural passage in the west wall. A spiral stair in the SE corner then led to the more thinly walled upper levels. The SW corner still retains parts of a parapet. This Power castle (also called Woodstown) is said to have been captured by Cromwell in 1649.

Dunhill Castle

Dungarvan Castle

Dunmore Castle

DUNMORE   S689006   C

On a promontory by Dunmore Bay is a round tower 10.6m in diameter over walls 2.6m thick with signs of a later building having adjoined it to the NW, and a base batter on the other sides. The entrance on the east is protected by a murder hole and flanked by a guard room and a mural stair up to the only surviving upper level.

FEDDANS   S363160

In 1641 this building about 14m by 9m was held by Jeffry Power. It was described as the "stump of a castle", which is how one might describe what remains now, a ground floor and loft under a former vault with the NW end wall missing. There are gunloops in the embrasures facing NE and SE and a latrine chute on the NE.

KILMANAHAN   S143192

There are no early references to this castle although the remains suggest a 13th century courtyard castle. It was held by Patrick Geoff in 1640. High walls enclose a bawn 35m by 30m perched on a cliff above the Suir. A modern house lies in the SW corner and a roofless 19th century mansion fills the NW corner, whilst the more vulnerable SE and NE corners have round towers about 6m in diameter. That at the SE is an impressive structure of four storeys adjoining a 16th or 17th century house within the corner. It has squinch arches between it and the east curtain wall, whilst not far north of it is a square tower which seems to have originally functioned as a gatehouse before being adapted as part of the house, a new gateway having been made in the south wall of the bawn.

Lisfinny Castle

Kilmanahan Castle

KNOCKMAON   X189933

The low north and west walls remain of a tower on a rock. There are traces of vaulting and buried footings of walls around a bawn to the NW. This FitzGerald castle first mentioned in 1440 was forfeited after their rebellion and granted to Sir Christopher Hatton. His tenant Alyson Dalton valiantly held the castle against repeated FitzGerald attacks in the 1590s. It later passed to Sir Richard Osborne and in 1645 was captured by a Confederate force led by Lord Castlehaven.

LISFINNY   X992945   D

After the Desmond Rebellion of 1579 this tower above the Bride River was granted to Sir Walter Raleigh. It was in a ruinous condition in 1641, when held by the Earl of Cork. It measures 12.6m by 9.2m and has vaults over the second and fourth of five storeys. The entrance in the south end wall is protected by a murder hole from a chamber reached by a mural stair from the western window embrasure of the lowest main room. From the head of this stair rises a spiral stair in the SW corner with a turret over the top of it at wall-walk level. The third and fourth storeys have tall rectangular loops, latrines in the SE corner and fireplaces in the east wall. The top storey had two light windows. A retaining wall close to the south and east sides may be part of a bawn.

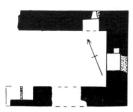

Feddans: plan

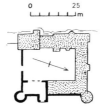

Kilmanahan: plan

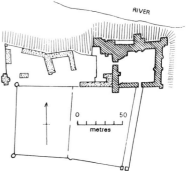

Lismore: plan

Dunmore: plan

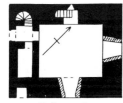

Lisfinny: plan

Lismore Castle

LISMORE   X047987   C

Prince John built a castle here above the Blackwater in 1185. It was soon destroyed but later rebuilt to provide a residence throughout the medieval period for the bishops of Lismore. It was damaged during the Desmond Rebellion of 1579 and later granted to Sir Walter Raleigh. After Raleigh's execution the castle passed to Sir Richard Boyle, who entirely rebuilt in it 1621. It had been described in 1600 as "broken and ruined" and no earlier work appears to survive. The castle withstood an eight day siege by the Confederate Catholics in 1643 during which the brewhouse wall was breached and was finally captured by them in 1645, being described as ruinous in the Down Survey of c1650. In the 1660s it was remodelled by the 2nd Earl of Cork, but was neglected during the 18th century. Four ranges enclose a court about 55m by 45m. The lower parts of the walls are 17th century but much of the upper parts and the majority of the features, and the present battlements and turrets date from a rebuilding begun in 1814 for the Dukes of Devonshire, who still own it. Original gunloops remain in the second and third storeys of the NE tower, and in a four storey circular tower on the west side, whilst the SE tower also has ancient work up as far as the third storey. Over a 12th century doorway on the south side plundered from St Mary's Church is the date 1615 and the motto "Gods Providence Is Our Inheritance". Also 17th century work is the spacious bawn to the south enclosed by a wall 3.5m high and 0.7m thick with an outer gateway of 1631-2 which was provided with new iron gates in 1643. See plan and photo on page 119 and page 11.

LOUGHDEHEEN   S528066   D

This castle was probably built by the Wyse family on lands which had formerly belonged to the Knights Hospitallers, and passed in the 17th century to the Sherlocks. An irregularly shaped platform roughly 50m square (now divided into three fields) has a retaining wall 1m thick rising up to 2.5m on the NE, SE and part of the SW sides. On the NW side is a 6m high gatehouse measuring 12.5m by 7.5m contained living room with a fireplace and latrine (and an attic above) over a passage (at the SW end) and a vaulted chamber with several double-splayed loops.

Loughdeheen Castle

Rathgormuck Castle

MOCOLLOP   X935994   D

The circular tower measuring 10.5m in diameter over walls 2.1m thick above a base batter only visible on the east could be 13th century work remodelled later, although the castle is not mentioned until 1462, when the 6th Earl of Desmond died within it. The tower was entered by means of an exterior stair up to a doorway into the west side of the second of five storeys, all circular rooms with the fourth one vaulted. The south and east parts of the tower are broken off above the stair curving up within the wall thickness. The existing ground level entrance is not ancient. The tower lay inside a small bawn said to have had a hall block filling its now-destroyed west end. The bawn has an east facing square gatehouse with a portcullis groove and drawbridge pit, and there are two other almost square flankers of later date with gunloops.

NORRISLAND   100975   D

The main block of the stronghouse owned in 1641 by William Greatrix (or Greatacres) is overgrown and very ruined but there remain parts of three small wings or corner turrets, that at the SW corner, which appears to be an addition, being the most complete.

PASSAGE EAST   S704102   A

A circular west corner flanker 5m in diameter with gunloops is the only relic of a fort built in c1590 beside an older blockhouse. It was captured by Cromwell in 1649.

RATHGORMUCK   S342180   D

After Nicholas Power's forfeiture in 1655 this tower was granted to Robert Davies. It measures 8.2m by 7.5m and has a wing 3m wide projecting from the south end of the west wall. The recess in the SE corner may have contained the stairs. The vault over the second storey loft stops short of the south wall since it would otherwise prevent the use of a door into the wing. The single room over the vault has three altered windows and a fireplace in the NE corner.

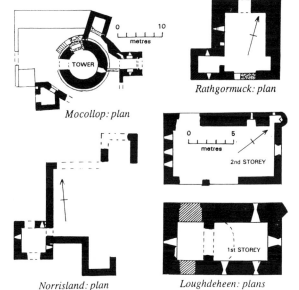

Mocollop: plan

Rathgormuck: plan

2nd STOREY

1st STOREY

Norrisland: plan

Loughdeheen: plans

Mocollop Castle

ROCKETT'S CASTLE or MAYFIELD or KNOCKANE   S480166

This 9.6m diameter round tower was held by Richard Strang in 1640 but passed to Sir Algernon May during the 1650s. It has a rebuilt parapet with a lookout and bellcote where the stairs terminate on the north side and machicolations on the east, south and west. The latter commands the pointed-arched entrance doorway which leads to a passage connecting with the stair, and having a guard-room on the south. The lowest room doorway is offset to the north, permitting the doorway to be commanded by a crossloop from that room. The third storey, over a vault, has a fireplace and three windows, one with a pair of ogival-headed lights. There are two more of these windows in the D-shaped fourth storey. The tower contains an engine and is covered by a water tank.

SHEANMORE   X957966   C

This tower measures 12.6m by 9.7m and contained a vaulted loft reached only by a hatch from the ground floor room below and an upper room with unusual double bartizans at the NW corner, there being separate machicolated chambers with gunloops projecting from the north and south walls very near the corner (and reached by a lintelled passage) rather than one bartizan upon the corner itself. This upper room has a fireplace and is reached by a stair in the north and east walls from one of the ground floor window embrasures. The south wall has a latrine chute from a now destroyed fourth storey. This FitzGerald castle was burnt in 1570 by the Earl of Ormond. After Maurice FitzGerald was forfeited in 1584 it was granted to Sir Walter Raleigh, but he leased it to Thomas Colthurst. In 1598 it was occupied by the Duffs and by 1640 it was held by Thomas Jackson.

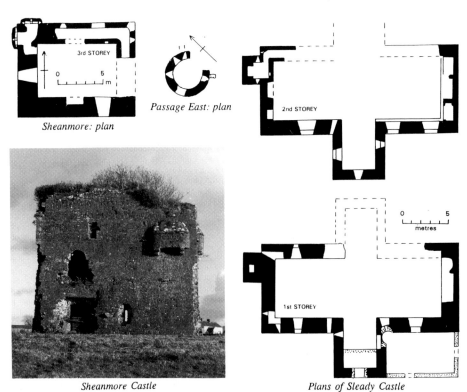

Sheanmore: plan

Passage East: plan

2nd STOREY

1st STOREY

Sheanmore Castle

Plans of Sleady Castle

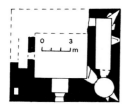

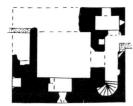

Templemichael; plans

Rockett's Castle

Passage East

Sleady Castle

SLEADY   X188018   D

The stronghouse built by Philip MacGrath in 1628 was originally cruciform but the wing in the middle of the north side, which contained the entrance, has been destroyed along with the main block north wall east of it. The rest still stands to a height of three storeys and an attic and measures 21.4m by 9.4m over walls up to 1.6m thick. There are fireplaces in the end walls and a latrine turret projects near the north end of the west wall. There is a bartizan on the NE corner.

STRANCALLY   X102860

A hall block measuring about 14m by 9.5m lies beside the west side of the Blackwater River. A stair in the north wall connects an upper chamber with seven window embrasures with a lower chamber with a basement under the east end which can only have been reached by ladder and trapdoor. A NW wing on a rock outcrop has been destroyed. On another rock outcrop higher up is a 5m high fragment with evidence of vaulting from a former tower house. The remains are overgrown and difficult to reach by land. This castle was held by James FitzJohn FitzGerald, executed for rebellion in 1579. It was granted to Sir Walter Raleigh in 1586 and by 1640 had passed into the possession of John Gillard. It was captured in 1645 by Lord Castlehaven and later passed to the Boyle earls of Cork.

TEMPLEMICHAEL   X069831   D

On a rise above the west side of the Blackwater is a 16th century FitzGerald castle said to have been attacked by Cromwell in 1649. It consists of a tower house now totally lacking its NW corner and a circular flanker of a bawn 5m in diameter just 4m away to the NE. The tower measures 12.4m by 11.3m and contains chambers over the entrance and adjoining guardroom in the 3.7m thick east wall, the doorway being covered by a gunloop and the passage through to the lowest room being dog-legged. The second storey was vaulted and had angle-loops off the mural room and the spiral stair in the SE corner (which also has a stirrup-shaped loop) and there was a latrine in the west wall. The fourth of the five storeys was also vaulted.

TICKINCOR   S240227   C

This stronghouse built by Alexander Power c1620 passed to Sir Thomas Stanley and then in the 1650s to Sir Nicholas Osborne. His descendants occupied the house until they moved to Newton Anner in Tipperary in the late 18th century. It consists of a main block of three storeys and an attic with a staircase wing projecting from the middle of the east side. In the 19th century the building was modified with new floors at different levels and a wide carriage entrance was pierced through where the entrance doorway was on the west side, which has two gables. There appear to have been short sections of open wall-walks at the corners and there is a gunloop in the stair wing. There are four fireplaces on the third storey. Two of the three chimneys upon the stair wing are false ones for the sake of symmetry.

TOURIN   X096965

This four storey tower measuring 11.6m by 8m has a blocked up ground floor fireplace in the east wall and no vaults over the main rooms, so it was probably fairly new in 1640 when Edward Gratrix occupied it as a tenant of Edmund Roche. It was later conveyed to John Nettles, and his grandson sold the castle to the Nettles family in 1780. The third and fourth storeys each have a fireplace and a mural chamber in the north end wall and two-light windows with hoodmoulds near the south end of the east and west walls. The top storey also has an ogival-headed south window and access into the SE corner bartizan, whilst the NW bartizan is reached from the wall-walk around an attic with a modern roof.

Reginald's Tower, Waterford

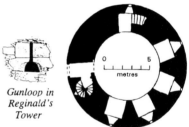

*Gunloop in
Reginald's
Tower*

Reginald's Tower: plan

Dungarvan Castle

Plan of Waterford City

Tourin Castle

Tickincor Castle

WATERFORD S611124 E

A triangular area on the south side of the Suir is thought to have been walled by the Danes in the 9th or 10th century. Of this part of the defences a 4m high and 400m length of towerless wall, probably of later date, remains along the south side. Nothing remains of the Colbeck Gate on the south or the Arundel Gate and Our Lady's Gate on the west side, nor of towers known St Martin's Castle and Keyser's Castle at the SW corner and midway along the north side (by the Post Office) respectively, nor of the circular NW corner tower known as Turgesius's Castle. However at the eastern end of the promontory site there still remains a circular keep 13.4m in diameter standing complete 15m high to the parapet enclosing a conical roof. Now a museum known as Reginald's Tower, but previously known as Dundory, this tower has walls 3m thick in the lower two levels probably dating from c1200, but thinner in the upper levels, which are a later medieval rebuilding. It was originally used as a prison and later as a mint. The tower was originally entered on the west side at second storey level, where there is a spiral staircase, but there are two inserted doorway on the east, one of which led to an adjoining oval platform or blockhouse with embrasures for eight guns added in the mid 16th century. The first and second storeys each have four window embrasures, a mural chamber or latrine and a fireplace. This building is said to have played a central part in the successful defence of the city against the Yorkist pretender Perkin Warbeck in 1495.

During the 13th century a larger area west and SW of the Danish town was additionally enclosed with walls. Remains (going clockwise from east to north) include lengths either side of Parnell St, a length east of Manor St between the 7m diameter Watch Tower and another round tower, a section by Castle St including the rectangular Double Tower, the D-shaped French Tower at the SW corner, a long section on west with the Semi-Lunate Tower, two other fragments leading round towards the square Beach Tower, and finally a small fragment just north of Great George's St. All the towers named here stand more-or-less to full height. The Watch Tower contains a stirrup-shaped loop. Nothing remains, however of the St John's Gate facing south, and the two western gates, Newgate and St Patrick's. Captain Edmund York is thought to have begun the still partly star-shaped fort outside St Patrick's Gate in the 1590s, although it was not completed until 1625. Commanding the whole city, it is now occupied by a police station. Another star-shaped fort is thought to have been begun in 1588 during the Armada scare, but later abandoned.

OTHER CASTLE REMAINS IN COUNTY WATERFORD

BALLYKEEROGE X327979 Shape of rubble on site suggests a stronghouse about 22m by 9m. Also had bawn. Granted to Sir Nicholas Walshe in 1587.

BALLYNAKILL S637109 Part of tower held by Dobbin family in 1640 in inhabited late 17th century house of two storeys and attic.

BALLYNATRAY X081831 Part of Richard Boyle's stronghouse is thought to remain in the basement of the late 18th century house.

BARNANKILE S308017 Only the west wall 3m high with three double-splayed loops remains of a stronghouse 19.6m by 6.9m. In 1640 it was described as a large slate house owned by Darby O'Brien of Kilcomeragh Castle.

CAMPHIRE X093929 Ruined and altered lowest stage of tower 12.5m by 10.0m near Blackwater. Spiral stair at SW and latrine chute on east at second storey.

CARROWNCASHLANE X258967 Lowest level only of tower 7.6m by 7m. Doorway on west side, where there is an irregularly shaped ditched enclosure.

COOLBUNIA S674119 Rubble pile beside house of square tower held c1640 by Sir Peter Aylward still two storeys high c1880. 3m high motte in woodland to west.

CROOKE S697089 SE corner only with traces of mural stair remains of a Power tower 13.2m by 9.5m with east doorway. Second storey had vault.

CURRAGHMORE S440154 Much altered Le Poer tower within NE side of courtyard house of c1700 belonging to Marquis of Waterford. NE forecourt of c1760.

DUAGH S589076 A platform 60m by 50m with traces of SW and SE bastions remains of a 16th or 17th century fort probably occupied as a barracks in 1798.

FOX'S CASTLE S343005 Base footings only remain of a tower recorded c1840.

GLEN S321232 The SW wall 10.5m long and 5m high alone survives. On the adjacent house is a stone dated 1676 with initials of Ian Francis Everard.

GLEN BEG X978987 House has Georgian facade but the three crow-stepped gabled wings and six chimney stacks suggest an early 17th century origin.

GREENAN S186216 Part of north wall with spiral stair adjoins crosswall with two doorways from long stronghouse said to have had a tower at the east end. Supposedly built in late 16th century by Edward Geogh. Adjoins possible motte site.

KILGAINY S227225 Low, thinly walled building lacking east wall. D-shaped projection to contain stair at SE corner. Held by Thomas Pendergast 1640.

KILNNACARRIGA X061941 4m high Z-shaped wall in farmyard on site of probable 17th century two storey stronghouse said to have measured about 14m by 7.5m.

LITTLE ISLAND S643117 FitzGerald tower about 14m by 10m on island in Suir held by James Walsh c1640 and now incorporated into late 19th century building.

NEWCASTLE S468080 Footings of Power family tower measuring 12m by 13m on rock.

MOTTES: Lismore X065986; Gallowshill X251932; Pembrokestown S535062.

CASTLE SITES IN COUNTY WATERFORD

ADAMSTOWN S252231 Site of assumed castle of Maurice Power in 1640.

AFFANE W108970 Site of 17th century stronghouse 13.5m by 6m.

CARRICKAHILLA X365999 Site of FitzGerald castle still existing in 1841.

CARRIGCASTLE S414018 Supposed site of castle on a rock outcrop.

CASTLE CONNAGH S169139 Former four storey tower with vaulted third storey by Nier River held by John Lee in 1640 and marked on Down Survey map of c1650.

CASTLEREAGH S205113 Site of late 16th century Power family castle.

CASTLETOWN S616051 Later ruin on site of house existing in 1640.

CLONKERDIN X150939 Site of castle marked on old maps.

CURRABAHA S376057 Supposed site of castle on promontory near Mahon river.

FURRALEIGH S350060 Site of probable FitzGerald castle.

GLENMORRISHMEEN S028986 Site of castle marked on map of 1773.

HACKETSTOWN X269826 Site of castle of Philip Rowe recorded c1640.

KILBREE X085990 Ruined 19h century house on site of stronghouse.

KILCOMERAGH S337057 Site of castle of Darby O'Brien recorded in 1640.
KILMACTHOMAS S395062 Site of castle marked on Down Survey map c1650.
KILMEADAN S525103 Later ruin on site of Power castle captured by Cromwell.
PILLTOWN X128803 Site of tower & bawn held by Sir Nicholas Walsh in 1640.
ROSS X465090 Site of a Power castle mentioned c1640.
CLONEA X945310 & FURRALEIGH S350060 are probable sites of FitzGerald castles.

A GLOSSARY OF TERMS

BARTIZAN - Turret corbelled out from a corner. BAWN - An enclosure, usually modest in size, surrounded by a wall. CORBEL - A projecting bracket supporting other stonework or timber beams. HALL-HOUSE - A two storey building containing a hall or chamber over a basement. HOODMOULD - Projecting moulding above an arch or lintel to throw off water. JAMB - The side of a doorway, window or other opening. KEEP - A citadel or ultimate strongpoint. The term is not medieval and such buildings were then called donjons. LIGHT - A compartment of a window. LOOP - A small opening to admit light or for the discharge of missiles. MACHICOLATION - A slot for dropping or shooting missiles at assailants. MULLION - A vertical member dividing the lights of a window. MURDER-HOLE - An internal machicolation, often in the vault of an entrance lobby. OGIVAL-ARCH - Arch of oriental origin with both convex and concave curves. PARAPET - A wall for protection at any sudden drop. PLINTH - The projecting base of a wall. PORTCULLIS - Wooden gate designed to rise and fall in vertical grooves, being hoisted up by a windlass. SCALE-AND-PLATT STAIRCASE - Staircase with short straight flights and turns at landings. SPANDREL - A surface between an arch and the rectangle containing it. STRONGHOUSE -A mansion capable of being defended against an attack. TOWER HOUSE - Self contained house with the main rooms stacked vertically. TRACERY - Intersecting ribwork in the upper part of a Gothic window. TRANSOM - A horizontal member dividing the lights of a window. WALL-WALK - A walkway protected by a parapet on top of a wall.

FURTHER READING

Castles in Ireland, Tom McNeil, 1997
Castles of County Cork, James N. Healy, 1988
The Medieval Castles of Ireland, David Sweetman, 1999
Irish Castles and Castellated Houses, Harold Leask, 1941
Guide to the National Monuments of Ireland, Peter Harbison, 1970
The Shell Guide to Ireland, Lord Killanin and Michael Duignan, 1969
Castles and Fortifications in Ireland 1485-1945, Paul Kerrigan, 1995
There are ancient monuments inventories published by the Office of Public Works available
    for Cork (4 vols - 1992 - 2000), and Waterford (1999). Two other archaeological
    inventories cover parts of Kerry - the peninsulars of Dingle (1986), and Iveragh (1996).
See also the annual proceedings of the Royal Irish Academy, and the Journals of the Cork
    Historical and Archaeological Society, the Royal Society of Antiquaries of Ireland.
Guide pamphlets, leaflets or monographs exist for: Barryscourt, Blarney and Ross

INDEX OF CASTLES